Lao-tzu's
Taoteching

Lao-tzu's
Taoteching

THE WAY

translated by Red Pine
with selected commentaries
of the past 2000 years

Published in the United States of America by Mercury House, San Francisco, California, a nonprofit publishing company devoted to the free exchange of ideas and guided by a dedication to literary values.

UNITED STATES CONSTITUTION, FIRST AMENDMENT: Congress shall make no law respecting an establishment of religion, or prohibiting the free exercise thereof; or abridging the freedom of speech, or of the press; or the right of the people peaceably to assemble, and to petition the Government for a redress of grievances.

Manufactured in the United States of America.

LIBRARY OF CONGRESS
CATALOGUING-IN-PUBLICATION DATA
Lao-tzu.
[Tao te ching. English]
Lao-tzu's Taoteching / translated by Red Pine,
with selected commentaries of the past 2000 years.
p. cm.
ISBN 1-56279-085-4 (pbk.)
I. Pine, Red. II. Title.
BL1900.L26E513 1996
299´.51482—DC20   96-18579
CIP

FIRST EDITION
10 12 14 16 18 20 19 17 15 13 11
2 4 6 8 9 7 5 3 1

for
Ku Lien-chang

Contents

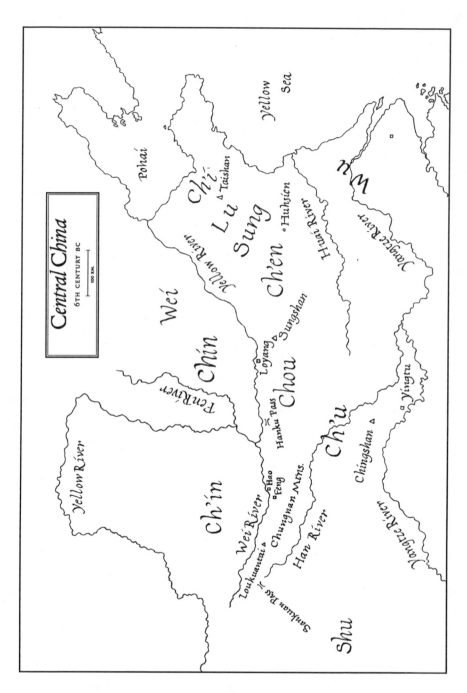

Central China in the sixth century BC. Map by Paul Hansen.

Introduction

The *Taoteching* is at heart a simple book. Written at the end of the sixth century BC by a man called Lao-tzu, it is a vision of what our lives would be like if we were more like the dark, new moon.

Lao-tzu teaches us that the dark can always become light and contains within itself the potential for growth and long life, while the light can only become dark and brings with it decay and early death. Lao-tzu chose long life. Thus he chose the dark.

The word that Lao-tzu chose to represent this vision was *Tao* 道. But *Tao* means "road" or "way" and doesn't appear to have anything to do with darkness. The character is made up of two graphs: "首: head" and "辶: go." To make sense of how the character came to be constructed, early Chinese philologists concluded that "head" must mean the start of something and that the two graphs together show someone starting on a trip. But a Chinese scholar in Taiwan has recently presented a novel, and more convincing, interpretation of the word's origins. According to Tu Er-wei, the "head" in the character *tao* is the face of the moon. And the meaning of "road" comes from watching this disembodied face as it moves across the sky.

Tu also notes that *tao* shares a common linguistic heritage with words that mean "moon" in other cultures: Tibetans call the moon *da-ua;* the Miao, who now live in southwest China but who lived in the same state as Lao-tzu when he was alive, call it *tao-tie;* the ancient Egyptians called it *thoth.* Tu Er-wei could have also added *dar-sha,* which means "new moon" in Sanskrit.

However, the heart of Tu's thesis is not linguistic, but textual and based on references within the *Taoteching.* Lao-tzu says the Tao is between Heaven and Earth, it's Heaven's Gate, it's empty but inexhaustible, it doesn't die, it waxes and wanes, it's distant and dark, it doesn't try to be full, it's the light that doesn't blind, it has thirty spokes and two thirteen-day (visible) phases, it can be strung like a bow or expand and contract like a bellows, it moves the other way (in relation to the sun), it's the great image, the hidden immortal, the crescent soul, the dark union, the dark womb, the dark beyond dark. If this isn't the moon, what is it?

Tu Er-wei has, I think, uncovered a deep and primitive layer of the *Taoteching* that has escaped the attention of other scholars. Of course, we cannot say for certain that Lao-tzu was consciously aware of the Tao's association with the moon. But we have his images, and they are too often lunar to dismiss as accidental.

In associating the Tao with the moon, Lao-tzu was not alone. The symbol Taoists have used since ancient times to represent the Tao ☯ shows the two conjoined phases of the moon. And how could they ignore such an obvious connection between its cycle of change and our own? Every month we watch the moon grow from nothing to a luminous disc that scatters the stars and pulls the tides within us all. The oceans feel it. The earth feels it. Plants and animals feel it. Humans also feel it, though it is women who seem to be most aware of it. In the *Huangti Neiching,* or *Yellow Emperor's Internal Book of Medicine,* Ch'i Po explained to the Yellow Emperor: "When the moon begins to grow, blood and breath begin to surge. When the moon is completely full, blood and breath are at their fullest, tendons and muscles are at their strongest. When the moon is completely empty, tendons and muscles are at their weakest" (8.26).

The advance of civilization has separated us from this easy lunar awareness. We call people affected by the moon "lunatics," making clear our disdain for its power. Lao-tzu redirects our vision to this ancient mirror. But instead of pointing to its light, he points to its darkness. Every month the moon effortlessly shows us that something comes from nothing. Lao-tzu asks us to emulate this aspect of the moon, not the full moon, which is destined to wane, but the new moon, which holds the promise of rebirth. And while he has us gazing at the moon's dark mirror, he asks why we don't we live longer than we do. After all, don't we share the same nature as the moon, and isn't the moon immortal?

Scholars tend to ignore Lao-tzu's emphasis on darkness and immortality, for it takes the book beyond the reach of academic analysis. For them, darkness is just a more poetic way of describing the mysterious. And immortality is a euphemism for long life. Over the years, they have distilled what they call Lao-tzu's "Taoist philosophy" from the later developments of "Taoist religion." They call the *Taoteching* a treatise on political or military strategy, or they see it as primitive scientific naturalism or utopianism—or just a bunch of sayings.

But trying to force the *Taoteching* into the categories of modern discourse not only distorts the *Taoteching,* it also treats the traditions that later Taoists have associated with the text as irrelevant and misguided. Meanwhile, the *Taoteching* continues to inspire millions of Chinese as a spiritual text, and I have tried to present it in that dark light. The words of philosophers fail here. If words are of any use at all, they are the words of the poet. For poetry has the ability to point us toward the truth and then stand aside, while prose stands in the doorway relating all the wonders on the other side but rarely lets us pass.

In this respect, the *Taoteching* is unique among the great literary works of the Chou dynasty. Aside from the anonymous poems and folksongs of the *Shihching*, or *Book of Odes*, we have no other poetic work from this early period of Chinese history; the wisdom of other sages was conveyed in prose. Although I haven't attempted to reproduce Lao-tzu's poetic devices (Hsu Yung-chang identifies twenty-eight different kinds of rhyme), I have tried to convey the poetic feel with which he strings together images for our breath and spirit, but not necessarily our minds. For the *Taoteching* is one long poem written in praise of something we cannot name, much less imagine.

Despite the elusiveness and namelessness of the Tao, Lao-tzu tells us we can approach it through *Te. Te* means "virtue," both in the sense of "moral character" as well as "power to act." Yen Ling-feng says, "Virtue is the manifestation of the Way. The Way is what Virtue contains. Without the Way, Virtue would have no power. Without Virtue, the Way would have no appearance" (*Taoteching*, 21). Han Fei put it more simply: "Te is the Tao at work" (*Taoteching*, 38). Te is our entrance to the Tao. Te is what we cultivate. Lao-tzu's Virtue, however, isn't the virtue of adhering to a moral code but action that involves no moral code, no self, no other—no action.

These are the two poles around which the *Taoteching* turns: the Tao, the dark, the body, the essence, the Way; and Te, the light, the function, the spirit, Virtue. In terms of origin, the Tao comes first. In terms of practice, Te comes first. The dark gives the light a place to shine. The light allows us to see the dark. But too much light blinds. Lao-tzu saw everyone chasing the light and hastening their own destruction. He encouraged people to choose the dark instead of the light, less instead of more, weakness instead of strength, inaction instead of action. What could be simpler?

Lao-tzu's preference for darkness extended to himself as well. For the past 2,500 years, the Chinese have revered the *Taoteching* as they have no other book, and yet they know next to nothing about its author. What they do know, or think they know, is contained in a brief biographical sketch included by Ssu-ma Ch'ien in a history of ancient China that he completed around 100 BC. Although we don't know what Ssu-ma Ch'ien's sources of information were, we do know he was considered the most widely travelled man of his age, and he

Village of Chujen east of Huhsien. Lao-tzu's old home was located on this, the fifth of nine bends of a canal that once enabled small boats to travel via adjoining waterways to the Yellow River to the north or the Huai River to the south. Photo by Bill Porter.

went to great lengths to verify the information he used. Of late it has become popular, if not *de rigueur,* to debunk his account of Lao-tzu, but it remains the earliest account we have and is worth repeating.

According to Ssu-ma Ch'ien, Lao-tzu was a native of Huhsien Prefecture in the state of Ch'u. Nowadays, the former prefectural town of Huhsien is called Luyi. If you are travelling in China, or simply want to find it on a map, look for the town of Shangchiu on the train line that runs between the city of Cheng-chou on the Yellow River and the Grand Canal town of Hsuchou. Luyi is about 70 kilometers south of Shangchiu. The shrine that marks the site of Lao-tzu's former village is just east of town.

The region is known as the Huang-Huai Plain. As its name suggests, it is the result of the regular flooding of the Huangho, or Yellow River, to the north and the Huaiho, or Huai River, to the south. The Chinese have been growing wheat and millet here since neolithic times, and more recently cotton and to-bacco. It remains one of the most productive agricultural areas in all of China, and it was a rich prize over which many states fought in ancient times.

Lao-tzu was born on this plain in 604 BC, or 571 BC, depending on which account of later historians we accept. Ssu-ma Ch'ien doesn't give us a date, but he does say that Huhsien was part of the great state of Ch'u. Officially, Huhsien belonged to the small state of Ch'en until 479 BC, when Ch'u eliminated Ch'en as a state once and for all. Some scholars have interpreted this to mean that either Huhsien did not belong to Ch'u when Lao-tzu was alive or that he must have been born there after 479 BC. But we need not accept either conclusion. Ssu-ma Ch'ien would have been aware that Ch'u controlled the fortunes of Ch'en as early as 598 BC, when Ch'u briefly annexed the entire state and then changed its mind, allowing Ch'en to exist as a "neighbor state."

Whether or not Huhsien was actually part of Ch'u is not important. What is important is that during the sixth century BC Ch'u controlled the region of which Huhsien was a part. This is significant not for verifying the accuracy of Ssu-ma Ch'ien's account but for directing our attention to the cultural influence that Ch'u represented. Ch'u was not like the other states in the central plains.

Although the rulers of Ch'u traced their ancestry to a grandson of the Yellow Emperor, the patriarch of Chinese culture, they represented its shamanistic periphery. From their ancestral home in the Sungshan area, just south of the Yellow River, they moved, or were pushed, steadily southwest, eventually ending up in the Chingshan area, just north of the Yangtze. Over the centuries they mixed with other tribal groups, such as the Miao, and incorporated elements of their shamanistic cultures. The Ch'u rulers took for their surname the word *hsiung,* meaning "bear," and they called themselves Man or Yi, which the Chinese in the central states interpreted to mean "barbarians."

The influence of Ch'u's culture on Lao-tzu is impossible to determine, but it does help us better understand the *Taoteching* knowing that it was written by a man who was no stranger to shamanistic conceptions of the sacred world. Certainly as Taoism developed in later centuries, it remained heavily indebted to shamanism, and some scholars see evidence of the Ch'u dialect in the *Taoteching* itself.

This, then, was the region where Lao-tzu grew up. But his name was not Lao-tzu (which means "Old Master"). Ssu-ma Ch'ien says his family name was Li, his personal name was Erh (meaning "ear," and hence, learned), and his posthumous name was Tan (meaning "long-eared," and hence, wise). In addition to providing us with a complete set of names, Ssu-ma Ch'ien also tells us that Lao-tzu, or Li Erh, served as Keeper of the Royal Archives.

Before continuing, I should note that some scholars reject Ssu-ma Ch'ien's Li Erh or Li Tan and suggest instead a man named Lao Tan, who also served as Keeper of the Royal Archives, but in the fourth century BC rather than the sixth century. Some find this later date more acceptable in explaining Lao-tzu's innovative literary style as well as in explaining why Chuang-tzu attributes passages of the *Taoteching* to Lao Tan but not Li Tan. For his part, Ssu-ma Ch'ien was certainly familiar with Chuang-tzu's writings, and he was not unaware of the fourth-century historian Lao Tan. In fact, he admits that some people thought that Lao Tan was Lao-tzu. But Ssu-ma Ch'ien was not convinced that the two were the same man. After all, if Tan was Lao-tzu's posthumous name, why shouldn't Chuang-tzu and other later writers call him "Old Tan"? And why couldn't there be two record keepers with the same name in the course of two centuries? If China's Grand Historian was not convinced that the fourth-century historian was the author of the *Taoteching*—certainly he had more documents at his disposal than we now possess—I see no reason to decide in favor of a man whose only claim to fame was to prophesy the ascendency of the state of Ch'in, which was to bring the Chou dynasty to an end in 221 BC. Meanwhile, I think I hear Lao-tzu laughing.

In any case, the place where Lao-tzu kept the archives was the Chou dynasty capital of Loyang, which was about 300 kilometers west of Huhsien. Loyang was a neolithic campsite as early as 3000 BC and a military garrison during the first dynasties: the Hsia and Shang. When the state of Chou overthrew the Shang dynasty in 1122 BC, the Duke of Chou built a new subsidiary capital around the old garrison. He dubbed it *Wangcheng*: City of the King. Usually, though, the king lived in one of the new dynasty's two western capitals of Feng and Hao, near modern Sian. But when these were destroyed in 771 BC, Wangcheng became the sole royal residence. And this is where Lao-tzu spent his time recording the events at court.

Lao-tzu must have been busy in the years following the death of King Ching. When King Ching died in 520 BC, two of his sons, Prince Chao and Prince Ching, both declared themselves his successor. At first Prince Chao gained the upper hand, and Prince Ching was forced to leave the capital. But with the help of other nobles, Prince Ching soon returned and established another capital fifteen kilometers to the east of Wangcheng, which he dubbed *Chengchou*: Glory of Chou. And in 516 BC, Prince Ching finally succeeded in driving his brother from the old capital.

In the same year, the Keeper of the Royal Archives, which were still in Wangcheng, received a visitor from the state of Lu. The visitor was a young man named K'ung Fu-tzu, or Confucius. Confucius was interested in ritual and asked Lao-tzu about the ceremonies of the ancient kings.

According to Ssu-ma Ch'ien, Lao-tzu responded with this advice: "The ancients you admire have been in the ground a long time. Their bones have turned to dust. Only their words remain. Those among them who were wise rode in carriages when times were good and slipped quietly away when times were bad. I have heard that the clever merchant hides his wealth so his store looks empty and that the superior man acts dumb so he can avoid calling attention to himself. I advise you to get rid of your excessive pride and ambition. They won't do you any good. This is all I have to say to you." Afterwards, Confucius told his disciples, "Today when I met Lao-tzu, it was like meeting a dragon."

The story of this meeting appears in a sufficient number of ancient texts to make it unlikely that it was invented by Taoists. Confucian records also report it taking place. According to the traditional account, Lao-tzu was eighty-eight years old when he met Confucius. If so, and if he was born in 604 BC, the two sages would have met in 516 BC, and Confucius would have been thirty-five. So it is possible. Though Confucius would not have had many disciples at such an early date.

Following his meeting with Confucius, Lao-tzu decided to take his own advice, and he left the capital by ox-cart. And he had good reason to leave. For when Prince Chao was banished from Wangcheng, he took with him the royal archives, the same archives of which Lao-tzu was supposedly in charge. If Lao-tzu needed a reason to leave, he certainly had one in 516 BC.

With the loss of the archives, Lao-tzu was out of a job. He was also, no doubt, fed up with the prospects for enlightened rule in the Middle Kingdom. Hence, he headed not for his hometown of Huhsien to the east but for Hanku Pass, which was 150 kilometers west of Loyang, and which served as the border between the Chou dynasty's central states and the semi-barbarian state of Ch'in, which now controlled the area surrounding the dynasty's former western capitals.

As Keeper of the Royal Archives, Lao-tzu no doubt supplied himself with the necessary documents to get through what was the most strategic pass in all of China. Hardly wide enough for two carts, it forms a seventeen-kilometer-long defile through a plateau of loess that has blown down from the north and accumulated between the Chungnan Mountains and the Yellow River over the past million years. In ancient times, the Chinese said that whoever controlled Hanku Pass controlled China. It was so easy to defend that during the Second World War the Japanese army failed to break through it, despite finding no difficulty in sweeping Chinese forces from the plains to the east.

Fortunately, Lao-tzu was expected. According to Taoist records, Master Yin Hsi was studying the heavens far to the west at the royal observatory at

*Hanku Pass. Midway between the Chou dynasty's eastern and western capitals
and situated between the Yellow River and the Chungnan Mountains. This
is where Lao-tzu met Yin Hsi, Warden of the Pass. Photo by Bill Porter.*

Loukuantai, when he noticed a purple vapor drifting from the east. He deduced that a sage would soon be passing through the area, and he knew that anyone travelling west would have to come through Hanku Pass. Hence he proceeded to the pass.

Ssu-ma Ch'ien, however, says Yin Hsi was Warden of the Pass and makes no mention of his association with Loukuantai. When Lao-tzu appeared, Yin Hsi recognized the sage and asked for instruction. According to Ssu-ma Ch'ien, Lao-tzu gave Yin Hsi the *Taoteching* and then continued on to distant, unknown realms.

Taoists agree that Lao-tzu continued on from Hanku Pass, but in the company of Yin Hsi, who invited him to his observatory 250 kilometers to the west. Taoists say Lao-tzu stopped long enough at Loukuantai to convey the teachings that make up his *Taoteching* and then travelled on through Sankuan Pass, another 150 kilometers to the west, and into the state of Shu. Shu was founded by a branch of the same lineage that founded the state of Ch'u, although its rulers revered the cuckoo rather than the bear. And in the land of the cuckoo, Lao-tzu finally achieved anonymity as well as immortality.

Loukuantai. The small knoll beyond the gravel bed of the Tien River and at the foot of the Chungnan Mountains is where Taoists say Lao-tzu wrote the Taoteching. *Photo by Bill Porter.*

Curiously, about six kilometers west of Loukuantai, there's a tombstone with Lao-tzu's name on it. The Red Guards knocked it down in the 1960s, and when I last visited Loukuantai in 1993 it was still down. I asked Loukuantai's abbot, Jen Fa-jung, what happened to Lao-tzu. Did he continue on through Sankuan Pass, or was he buried at Loukuantai? Master Jen suggested both stories were true. As Confucius noted, Lao-tzu was a dragon among men. And being a member of the serpent family, why should we wonder at his ability to leave his skin behind and continue on through cloud-barred passes?

And so, Lao-tzu, whoever he was and whenever he lived, disappeared and left behind his small book. The book at first didn't have a name. When writers like Mo-tzu and Wen-tzu quoted from it in the fifth century BC, or Chuang-tzu and Lieh-tzu quoted from it in the fourth century BC, or Han Fei explained passages in the third century BC and Huai-nan-tzu in the second century BC, they simply said "Lao-tzu says this" or "Lao Tan says that." And so people started calling the source of all these quotes *Laotzu*.

Ssu-ma Ch'ien also mentioned no name. He only said that Lao-tzu wrote a book, and it was divided into two parts. About the same time, people started calling these two parts *The Way* and *Virtue,* after the first lines of verses 1 and 38. And to these, were added the honorific *ching,* meaning "ancient text." And so Lao-tzu's book was called the *Taoteching,* the *Book of Tao and Te.*

In addition to its two parts, it was also divided into separate verses. But, as with other ancient texts, punctuation and enumeration of passages were left up to the reader. About the same time that Ssu-ma Ch'ien wrote his biography of Lao-tzu and people started calling the book the *Taoteching,* Yen Tsun produced a commentary in the first century BC that divided the text into seventy-two verses. A century earlier, or a couple of centuries later, no one knows which, Ho-shang Kung divided the same basic text into eighty-one verses. And a thousand years later, Wu Ch'eng tried a sixty-eight-verse division. But the system that has persisted through the centuries is that of Ho-shang Kung, who also gave each verse its own title.

The text itself has seen dozens of editions containing anywhere from five to six thousand characters. The numerical discrepancy is not as significant as it might appear and is largely the result of adding certain grammatical particles for clarity or omitting them for brevity. The greatest difference among editions centers not on the number of characters but on the rendering of certain phrases and the presence or absence of certain lines.

Over the centuries, several emperors have taken it upon themselves to resolve disputes concerning the choice among these variants. And the creation of a standard edition has resulted from their efforts. The standard edition, however, is still open to revision, and every student of the *Taoteching* repeats the process of choosing among variants to understand the text.

In this regard, *Taoteching* studies were blessed in late 1973 with the discovery of two copies of the text in a tomb that was sealed in 168 BC in a suburb of the provincial capital of Changsha known as Mawangtui. Despite the lapse of over 2,100 years, the copies, written on silk, were in remarkably good condition.

Kao Chih-hsi, who supervised their removal and who directed the Mawangtui Museum until just recently, attributes their preservation to layers of clay and charcoal that covered the tomb. At least this is his official explanation. In private, he says their preservation could have also been due to the presence of an unknown gas created by the decomposition of certain substances inside the tomb. He tried to take a sample of the gas, but the discovery was made in the middle of the Cultural Revolution, and he spent two days peddling his bicycle around Changsha before he found anyone who would loan him the necessary equipment. By then the gas was gone.

The books, though, made up for his disappointment. Along with the *Taoteching* there were several hitherto unknown commentaries on the *Yiching*

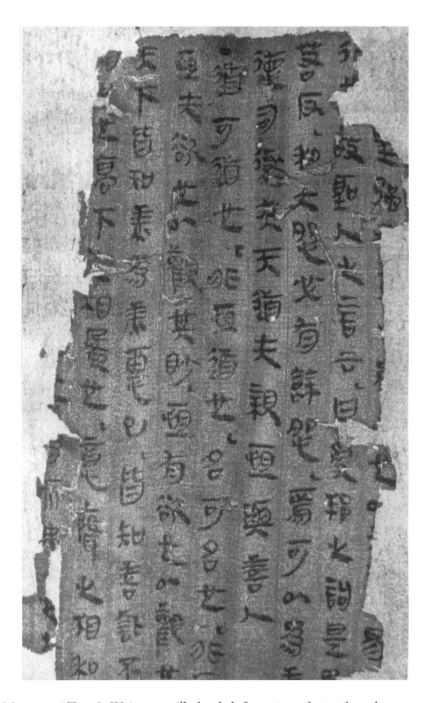

Mawangtui Text A. Written on silk shortly before 206 BC, the text here shows verse 1 following verse 79, an arrangement unique to the Mawangtui texts.
Photo by Steven R. Johnson.

as well as a number of lost texts attributed to the Yellow Emperor. The Chinese Academy of Sciences immediately convened a committee of scholars to examine these texts and decipher illegible sections.

In the years since their discovery, the two Mawangtui copies of the *Taoteching* have contributed greatly to the elucidation of a number of difficult and previously misunderstood passages. Without them, I would have been forced to choose among unsatisfactory variants on too many occasions. Still, the Mawangtui texts contain numerous omissions and errors and need to be used with great care.

Fortunately, we also have another text that dates from the same period. Like the Mawangtui texts, it was discovered in a tomb that was sealed shortly after 200 BC. This tomb was located near the Grand Canal town of Hsuchou and was opened in 574 AD. Not long afterward, the court astrologer Fu Yi published an edition of the copy of the *Taoteching* that was found inside.

In addition to the Mawangtui and Fuyi texts, we also have more than sixty copies of the text that were found shortly after 1900 in the Silk Road oasis of Tunhuang. Most of these copies date from the eighth and ninth centuries. However, one of them was written by a man named Suo Tan in 270 AD, giving us yet another early hand-written edition to consider.

We also have a copy of the *Taoteching* written by the great fourth-century calligrapher Wang Hsi-chih, as well as a dozen or so stelae on which various emperors had the entire text carved. Finally, we have the text as it appears in such early commentaries as those of Yen Tsun, Ho-shang Kung, and Wang Pi (not to mention numerous passages quoted in the ancient works of Mo-tzu, Wen-tzu, Chuang-tzu, Lieh-tzu, Han Fei, Huai-nan-tzu, and others).

In undertaking this translation, I have consulted nearly all of these editions and have produced a new recension incorporating my choices among the readings. For the benefit of those able to read Chinese, I have included the resulting text with my translation. I have also added a number of commentaries.

Over the centuries, some of China's greatest writers have devoted themselves to explaining the *Taoteching*, and no Chinese would think of reading the text without the help of at least one of these line-by-line or verse-by-verse explanations. When I first decided to translate the *Taoteching*, it occurred to me that Western readers are at a serious disadvantage without the help of such materials. To remedy this situation, I have collected several dozen of the better-known commentaries along with a few that are more obscure, and I have selected from among them those passages that provide important background information or insights.

Among the commentaries consulted, the majority of my selections come from a group of eleven men and one woman. In order of frequency, they include: Su Ch'e, Ho-shang Kung, Wu Ch'eng, Wang Pi, Te-ch'ing, Sung Ch'ang-hsing, Li Hsi-chai, Lu Hui-ch'ing, Wang P'ang, Ch'eng Hsuan-ying, the Taoist nun Ts'ao Tao-ch'ung, and Wang An-shih. For biographical information on these and other commentators, readers are directed to the glossary at the back of this book (page 165).

Readers will also notice that I have restricted the comments to what could fit on facing pages. The reason for this is that I envisioned this book as a discussion between Lao-tzu and a group of people who have thought deeply about his text. And I wanted to have everyone in the same room rather than in adjoining suites.

I have also added a few remarks of my own, though I have usually limited these to textual issues. In this regard, I have tried to restrict myself to those lines where my choice among variants may have resulted in a significant departure from other translations that readers might have in their possession. The *Taoteching* is, after all, one of the most translated books in the world, exceeded only by the *Bible* and the *Bhagavad-Gita*.

Since the text first appeared in Latin in 1788, more than a hundred translations have been published in Western languages alone, and readers could not be blamed for wondering if there isn't something inherent in the text that infects those who read it with the desire to produce even more translations.

My own attempt to add to this number dates back nearly twenty-five years to when I attended a course in Taiwan given by John C.H. Wu. Professor Wu had himself produced an excellent English translation of the *Taoteching*, and he offered a course on the subject to graduate students in the philosophy department at the College of Chinese Culture, which I was attending between stays at Buddhist temples.

Once a week, about six of us filed past the guards at the stately Chung-shanlou on Yangmingshan, where the government had provided Professor Wu with a bungalow in recognition of his long service to the country. In addition to translating the *Taoteching*, Professor Wu also translated the *New Testament* and drafted his country's constitution, as well as served as China's ambassador to the Vatican and its chief representative to the Hague. Once a week, we sipped tea, ate his wife's cookies, and discussed a verse or two of Lao-tzu's text. Between classes, I tried translating the odd line in the margins of Professor Wu's bilingual edition, but I did not get far. After one semester, the course ended, and I moved to a Buddhist monastery in the hills south of Taipei, where

I put aside Lao-tzu's text in favor of Buddhist sutras and poetry. But ever since then, I have been waiting for an opportunity to dust off this thinnest of ancient books and resume my earlier attempt at translation.

The opportunity finally presented itself when I recently returned to America after more than twenty years in Taiwan and Hong Kong. In the early seventies, when I was attending graduate school at Columbia University, I recall Professor Bielenstein quoting W.A.C.H. Dobson, who said it was time for a Sinologist to retire when he announced he was working on a new translation of the *Taoteching*. And so I have joined the ranks of the retired.

I don't know if Dobson would have approved. His remarks, I suspect, were intended more as friendly criticism of the presumption that translating the *Taoteching* entails. Though relatively brief, the *Taoteching* is a difficult text. But it is also a transparent one.

For the past two years, one image that has repeatedly come to mind while working on this translation is skating on a newly frozen lake near my home in Idaho when I was a boy. Sometimes the ice was so clear, I felt like I was skating across the night sky, and the only sounds I could hear were the cracks that echoed through the dark, transparent depths. I thought if the ice ever gave way I would find myself on the other side of the universe, and I always carried ice picks just in case I had to pull myself out. The ice never broke. But I've been hearing those cracks again.

Red Pine
Port Townsend, Washington
First Quarter, Last Moon, Year of the Pig

Lao-tzu's
Taoteching

Statue of Lao-tzu at Cinnabar Cauldron,
Loukuantai. Photo by
Bill Porter.

1

道可道。非恆道。名可名。非恆名。無名
天地之始。有名萬物之母。故恆無欲以觀
其眇。恆有欲以觀其徼。此兩者同。出而
異名。同謂之玄。玄之又玄。眾眇之門。

The way that becomes a way

is not the Immortal Way

the name that becomes a name

is not the Immortal Name

the maiden of Heaven and Earth has no name

the mother of all things has a name

thus in innocence we see the beginning

in passion we see the end

two different names

for one and the same

the one we call dark

the dark beyond dark

the door to all beginnings

The word *tao* means "road" or "way" and, by extension, "way of doing something." TU ER-WEI says, "*Tao* originally meant 'moon.' The *Yiching*: 42, 52 stresses the bright moon, while Lao-tzu stresses the dark moon" (pg. ii–iii).

CONFUCIUS says, "The Tao is what we can never leave. If we can leave it, it isn't the Tao" (*Chungyung*: 1).

HO-SHANG KUNG says, "What we call a way is a moral or political code, while the Immortal Way takes care of the spirit without effort and brings peace to the world without struggle. It conceals its light and hides its tracks and can't be called a way. As for the Immortal Name, it's like a pearl inside an oyster, a piece of jade inside a rock: shiny on the inside and dull on the outside."

CH'ENG CHU says, "A sage doesn't reveal the Way, not because he keeps it secret, but because it can't be revealed. Hence his words are like footsteps that leave no tracks."

THE BUDDHA says, "He who says I teach the Dharma maligns me. Who teaches the Dharma teaches nothing" (*Diamond Sutra*: 21).

LI HSI-CHAI says, "Things change but not the Tao. The Tao is immortal. It arrives without moving and comes without being called."

SU CH'E says, "The ways of kindness and justice change but not the way of the Tao. No name is its body. Name is its function. The sage embodies the Tao and uses it in the world. But while entering the myriad states of being, he remains in non-being."

WANG PI says, "From the infinitesimal all things develop. From nothing all things are born. When we are free of desire, we can see the infinitesimal where things begin. When we are subject to desire, we can see where things end. 'Two' refers to 'maiden' and 'mother.'"

TS'AO TAO-CH'UNG says, "'Two' refers to 'innocence' and 'passion,' or in other words, stillness and movement. Stillness corresponds to nonexistence. Movement corresponds to existence. Provisionally different, they are ultimately the same. Both meet in darkness."

THE SHUOWEN says, "*Hsuan:dark* means 'black with a bit of red in it,'" like the darker half of the *yin-yang* symbol. In Shensi province, where this text was written, doors are still painted black with a thin line of red trim. And every road begins with a door.

TE-CH'ING says, "Lao-tzu's philosophy is all here. The remaining five-thousand words only expand on this first verse."

The punctuation introduced by Ssu-ma Kuang and Wang An-shih in lines five through eight makes their subject *yu:being* and *wu:non-being*. But this is not supported by the grammatical particles of the Mawangtui texts. Also, in line five, *shih:maiden* normally means "beginning," but THE SHUOWEN says, "*Shih* means 'a virgin.'" MA HSU-LUN says *shih* is a loan word for the nearly identical *t'ai*. While *t'ai* normally means "fetus," the *Shuowen* says it means "a woman in her third month of pregnancy." Note, too, that a woman did not receive her public name until after marriage. In line seven, most editions have *miao:mysterious*. But PI YUAN says, "In ancient times there was no *miao:mysterious*, only *miao:small/beginning*," which is what we find in the Mawangtui texts.

2

天下皆知美。之為美。斯惡已。皆知善。之為善。斯不善已。有
無相生。難易相成。長短相形。高下相盈。音聲相和。先後相
隨。恆也。是以聖人處無為之事。行不言之教。萬物作焉而不
始。為而不恃。成功而不居。夫唯不居。是以不去。

All the world knows beauty
but if that becomes beautiful
this becomes ugly
all the world knows good
but if that becomes good
this becomes bad
the coexistence of have and have not
the coproduction of hard and easy
the correlation of long and short
the codependence of high and low
the correspondence of note and noise
the coordination of first and last
is endless
thus the sage performs effortless deeds
and teaches wordless lessons
he doesn't start all the things he begins
he doesn't presume on what he does
he doesn't claim what he achieves
and because he makes no claim
he suffers no loss

LU HSI-SHENG says, "What we call beautiful or ugly depends on our feelings. Nothing is necessarily beautiful or ugly until feelings make it so. But while feelings differ, they all come from our nature, and we all have the same nature. Hence the sage transforms his feelings and returns to his nature and thus becomes one again."

WU CH'ENG says, "The existence of things, the difficulty of affairs, the size of forms, the magnitude of power, the pitch and clarity of sound, the sequence of position, all involve contrasting pairs. When one is present, both are present. When one is absent, both are absent."

LU HUI-CH'ING says, "These six pairs all depend on time and occasion. None of them is eternal. The sage, however, acts according to the Immortal Tao, hence he acts without effort. And he teaches according to the Immortal Name, hence he teaches without words. Beautiful and ugly, good and bad don't enter his mind."

WANG WU-CHIU says, "The sage is not interested in deeds or words. He simply follows the natural pattern of things. Things rise, develop, and reach their end. This is their order."

WANG AN-SHIH says, "The sage creates but does not possess what he creates. He acts but does not presume on what he does. He succeeds but does not claim success. These three all result from selflessness. Because the sage is selfless, he does not lose his self. Because he does not lose his self, he does not lose others."

SU CH'E says, "Losing something is the result of claiming something. How can a person lose what he doesn't claim?"

LI HSI-CHAI says, "Lao-tzu's 5,000-word text clarifies what is mysterious as well as what is obvious. It can be used to attain the Tao, to order a country, or to cultivate the body."

HO-SHANG KUNG titles this verse "Cultivating the Body."

SUNG CH'ANG-HSING says, "Those who practice the Way put an end to distinctions, get rid of name and form, and make of themselves a home for the Way and Virtue."

I have incorporated line thirteen from the Mawangtui texts and have also used their wording of the six preceding lines. In line sixteen, I have relied on the Fuyi edition as well as Mawangtui Text B in reading *shih:start* in place of *tz'u:say/refuse.* I have followed the Mawangtui texts again in omitting the line "he doesn't possess what he begets" after line sixteen as an interpolation from verse 51. Lines seventeen and eighteen also appear in verse 77.

3

不上賢。使民不爭。不貴難得之貨。使民不為
盜。不見可欲。使民不亂。是以聖人之治。虛
其心。實其腹。弱其志。強其骨。恆使民無知
無欲。使夫知者不敢為。則無不治。

Bestowing no honors
keeps people from fighting
prizing no treasures
keeps people from stealing
displaying no attractions
keeps people from making trouble
thus the rule of the sage
empties the mind
but fills the stomach
weakens the will
but strengthens the bones
by keeping the people from knowing or wanting
and those who know from daring to act
he thus governs them all

SU CH'E says, "Bestowing honors embarrasses those who don't receive them to the point where they fight for them. Prizing treasures pains those who don't possess them to the point where they steal them. Displaying attractions distresses those who don't enjoy them to the point where they cause trouble. If people aren't shown these things, they won't know what to want and will cease wanting."

WANG CHEN says, "The sage empties the mind of reasoning and delusion, he fills the stomach with loyalty and honesty, he weakens the will with humility and compliance, and he strengthens the bones with what people already have within themselves."

WANG PI says, "Bones don't know how to make trouble. It's the will that creates disorder. When the mind is empty, the will is weak."

WANG P'ANG says, "An empty mind means no distinctions. A full stomach means no desires. A weak will means no external plans. Strong bones mean standing on one's own and remaining unmoved by outside forces. By bestowing no honors, the sage keeps people from knowing. By prizing no treasures, he keeps people from wanting."

LU NUNG-SHIH says, "The mind knows and chooses, while the stomach doesn't know but simply contains. The will wants and moves, while bones don't want but simply stand there. The sage empties what knows and fills what doesn't know, he weakens what wants and strengthens what doesn't want."

YEN TSUN says, "He empties his mind and calms his breath. He concentrates his essence and strengthens his spirit."

HUANG YUAN-CHI says, "The sage purifies his ears and eyes, puts an end to dissipation and selfishness, embraces the one, and empties his mind. An empty mind forms the basis for transmuting cinnabar by enabling us to use our *yang*-breath to transform our *yin*-essence. A full stomach represents our final form, in which our *yang*-breath gradually and completely replaces our *yin*-essence."

WEI YUAN says, "The reason the world is in disorder is because of action. Action comes from desire. And desire comes from knowledge. The sage doesn't talk about things that can be known or display things that can be desired. This is how he brings order to the world."

LIU CHING says, "This verse describes how the sage cultivates himself in order to transform others."

In the Fuyi edition and Tunhuang copy S.477, an additional line follows the "thus" of the last line: *wei-wu-wei:act without acting.* Commentators who accept this version often explain it with a quote from Confucius: "To govern without effort. That was Shun. And what did he do? All he did was face south and bow" (*Lunyu*: 15.4). I've used the Mawangtui texts, which omit this line. Lao-tzu's emphasis on the stomach over the eyes also appears in verse 12.

4

先。湛兮。似或存。吾不知其誰之子。象帝之宗。挫其銳。解其紛。和其光。同其塵。道沖。而用之。又不盈。淵兮。似萬物之

The Tao is so empty
those who use it
never become full again
and so deep
as if it were the ancestor of us all
dulling our edges
untying our tangles
softening our light
merging our dust
and so clear
as if it were present
I wonder whose child it is
it seems it was here before Ti

WANG AN-SHIH says, "The Tao possesses form and function. Its form is the original breath that doesn't move. Its function is the empty breath that alternates between Heaven and Earth."

WU CH'ENG says, "'Empty' means empty like a bowl. The Tao is essentially empty, and people who use it should be empty too. To be full is contrary to the Tao. 'Deep' means what cannot be measured. An ancestor unites a lineage just as the Tao unites all things. 'As if' suggests reluctance to compare."

LI HSI-CHAI says, "The ancient masters of the Way had no ambition, hence they dulled their edges and did not insist on anything. They had no fear, hence they untied every tangle and avoided nothing. They did not care about beauty, hence they softened their light and forgot about themselves. They did not hate ugliness, hence they merged with the dust and did not abandon others."

WEI YUAN says, "By taking advantage of edges, we create conflicts with others. By shining bright lights, we illuminate their dust. Grinding down edges makes conflicts disappear. Turning down lights merges dust with dust and dust with darkness."

HUANG YUAN-CHI says, "A person who can adjust his light to that of the crowd and merge with the dust of the world is like a magic mushroom among ordinary plants. You can't see it, but it makes everything smell better."

HSI T'UNG says, "The Tao is invisible. Hence Lao-tzu calls it 'clear.'"

THE SHUOWEN says, "*Chan:clear* means unseen."

LU NUNG-SHIH says, "'Clear' describes what is deep, what seems to be present and not to be present, what seems not to be present and not not to be present."

LIU CHING says, "If it's empty, it's deep. If it's deep, it's clear. The Tao comes from nothing. Hence the Tao is the child of nothing."

LI YUEH says, "Ti is the Lord of Creation. All of creation comes after Ti, except the Tao, which comes before. But the nature of the Tao is to yield, hence Lao-tzu doesn't insist it came before. Thus he says, 'it seems.'"

JEN CHI-YU says, "In ancient times no one denied the existence of Ti, and no one called his supremacy into doubt. Lao-tzu, however, says the Tao is 'the ancestor of all things,' which presumably included Ti as well" (pg. 34).

For such an enigmatic verse there are surprisingly few variants. In line three, I have gone along with the Fuyi edition, Tunhuang copy P.2584, and Mawangtui Text B in reading *yu-pu-ying:again-not-full* in place of *huo-pu-ying:maybe-not-full."* Because of problems created by their interpretation of the first four lines, some commentators think lines five through eight don't belong here. They do, in fact, reoccur in verse 56. I've read them as an explanation of the Tao's ancestral status, which makes kin of us all.

5

天地不仁。以萬物為芻狗。聖
人不仁。以百姓為芻狗。天地之
間。其猶橐蘥乎。虛而不屈。動而
愈出。多言數窮。不如守中。

Heaven and Earth are heartless
treating creatures like straw dogs
heartless is the sage
treating people like straw dogs
between Heaven and Earth
how like a bellows
empty but inexhaustible
each movement produces more
talking only wastes it
better to keep it inside

The Chinese characters *pu-jen:no heart* also refer to a fruit that has no seed or center.

HU SHIH says, "Lao-tzu's statement that Heaven and Earth are heartless undercut the ancient belief that Heaven and Man were of the same lineage and thereby created the basis for natural philosophy" (p. 56).

SU CH'E says, "Heaven and Earth aren't partial. They don't kill living things out of cruelty or give them birth out of kindness. We do the same when we make straw dogs to use in sacrifices. We dress them up and put them on the altar, but not because we love them. And when the ceremony is over, we throw them into the street, but not because we hate them. This is how the sage treats the people."

HUAI-NAN-TZU says, "When we make straw dogs or clay dragons, we paint them yellow and blue, decorate them with brocade, and tie red ribbons around them. The shaman puts on his black robe and the lord puts on his ceremonial hat to usher them in and to see them off. But once they've been used, they're nothing but clay and straw" (11). A similar description appears in *Chuangtzu*: 14.4.

WU CH'ENG says, "Straw dogs were used in praying for rain, and these particular bellows were used in metallurgy."

WANG P'ANG says, "A bellows is empty so that it can respond to things. Something moves, and it responds. It responds but retains nothing. Like Heaven and Earth in regard to the ten thousand things or the sage in regard to the people, it responds with what fits. It isn't tied to the present or attached to the past."

WANG AN-SHIH says, "The Tao has no substance or dimension, yet it works the breath of emptiness between Heaven and Earth and gives birth to the ten thousand things."

WANG TAO says, "The Tao cannot be talked about, yet we dismiss it as heartless. It cannot be named, yet we liken it to a bellows. Those who understand get the meaning and forget the words. Those who don't understand fail to see the truth and chatter away in vain."

HSIN TU-TZU says, "When the main path has many by-ways, sheep lose their way. When learning leads in many directions, students waste their lives" (*Liehtzu*: 8:25).

HO-SHANG KUNG says, "Whenever the mouth opens and the tongue moves, disaster is close behind. Better to guard your inner virtue, nurture your vital essence, protect your spirit, treasure your breath, and avoid talking too much."

SUNG CH'ANG-HSING says, "If our mouth doesn't talk too much, our spirit stays in our heart. If our ears don't hear too much, our essence stays in our genitals. In the course of time, essence becomes breath, breath becomes spirit, and spirit returns to emptiness.

The only textual variation here involves the appearance in both Mawangtui texts of *wen:hear* instead of the standard *yen:talk* in line nine. But since *wen:hear* was sometimes used for *wen:ask,* the meaning isn't significantly different, hence I've kept *yen:talk.*

6

浴神不死。是謂玄
牝。玄牝之門。是
謂天地之根。綿綿
今若存。用之不堇。

The valley spirit that doesn't die

we call the dark womb

the dark womb's mouth

we call the source of creation

as real as gossamer silk

and yet we can't exhaust it

THE SHANHAICHING says, "The Valley Spirit of Morning Light is a black and yellow, eight-footed, eight-tailed, eight-headed animal with a human face" (9). The *Shanhaiching*'s "valley spirit" is the moon, which runs ahead of the sun during the last eight days of its thirty-day cycle, lags behind during the first eight days, and faces the sun during its eight days of glory. For the remaining days of the month, it's too close to the sun to be visible. Like many other cultures, the ancient Chinese viewed the moon as the embodiment of the female element of creation.

WANG PI says, "The valley is what is in the middle, what contains nothing, no form, no shadow, no obstruction. It occupies the lowest point, remains motionless, and does not decay. All things depend on it for their development, but no one sees its shape."

YEN FU says, "Because it is empty, we call it a valley. Because there is no limit to its responsiveness, we call it a spirit. Because it is inexhaustible, we say it never dies. These three are the virtues of the Tao."

SU CH'E says, "A valley is empty but has form. A valley spirit is empty and has no form. What is empty and has no form is not alive. So how can it die? 'Valley spirit' refers to its virtue. 'Dark womb' refers to its capacity. This womb gives birth to the ten thousand things, and we call it dark because we see it give birth but not how it gives birth."

HSUEH HUI says, "The words Lao-tzu chooses are often determined by the demands of rhyme and should not be restricted to their primary meaning. Thus, *p'in:female animal* can also be read *p'in:womb*."

HO-SHANG KUNG says, "The valley is what nourishes. Someone who is able to nourish his spirit does not die. 'Spirit' means the spirits of the five organs: the gall bladder, the lungs, the heart, the kidneys, and the spleen. When these five organs are injured, the five spirits leave. 'Dark' refers to Heaven. In Man this means the nose, which links us with Heaven. 'Womb' refers to Earth. In Man this means the mouth, which links us with Earth. The breath that passes through our nose and mouth should be finer than gossamer silk and barely noticeable, as if it weren't actually present. It should be relaxed and never strained or exhausted."

WU CH'ENG says, "The empty valley is where spirits dwell, where breath isn't exhausted. Who relaxes their breath increases their vitality. Who strains their breath soon expires."

TE-CH'ING says, "Purposeful action leads to exhaustion. The Tao is empty and acts without purpose. Hence it can't be exhausted."

SUNG CH'ANG-HSING says, "The valley spirit, the dark womb, the source of creation, all act without acting. Just because we don't see them doesn't mean they don't exist."

LIU CHING says, "It's like the silk of a silkworm or the web of a spider: hard to distinguish, hard to grab. But then, it isn't Man that uses it. Only the spirit can use it."

TU TAO-CHIEN says, "This verse also appears in *Liehtzu: 1.1*, where it is attributed to the Yellow Emperor instead of Lao-tzu. Lao-tzu frequently incorporates passages from ancient texts. We see their traces in 'thus the sage proclaims' or 'hence the ancients say.' Thus Confucius said, 'I don't create. I only relate'" (*Lunyu:* 7.1).

LIEH-TZU says, "What creates life is not itself alive" (1.1).

7

天長地久。天地之所以能長且久者。以其不自生。故能長生。是以聖人退其身。而身先。外其身。而身存。不以其無私邪。故能成其私。

Heaven is eternal and Earth is immortal
the reason they're eternal and immortal
is because they don't live for themselves
hence they can live forever
thus the sage pulls himself back
but ends up in front
he lets himself go
but ends up safe
selflessness must be the reason
whatever he seeks he finds

CHU CH'IEN-CHIH says, "The line 'Heaven is eternal and Earth is immortal' was apparently an old saying, which Lao-tzu quotes in order to explain its significance."

CHIANG SSU-CH'I says, "'Heaven' refers to the point between the eyebrows. 'Earth' refers to the point just below the navel."

LU HUI-CH'ING says, "Heaven stands for the movement of time. Earth represents the transformation of form. Heaven and Earth have their origin in the dark womb. And the essence of the dark womb is the valley spirit that doesn't die. Because it doesn't die, it isn't born. Only what isn't born can give birth to the living. And because it doesn't give birth to itself, it can live forever."

TS'AO TAO-CH'UNG says, "What is not alive is the basis for life. By equating life and death, we are no longer burdened by life and death. By abandoning bodily form, we are no longer hindered by bodily form."

WU CH'ENG says, "To pull back means to be humble and not to try to be in front of others. To let go means to be content and not to try to add to our life. To find what one seeks means to be in front and safe."

SUNG CH'ANG-HSING says, "Heaven and Earth help creatures fulfill their needs by not having any needs of their own. Can the sage do otherwise? By following the Way of Heaven and Earth, the sage is revered by all and harmed by none. Hence he, too, lives long."

JEN FA-JUNG says, "The sage does not purposely seek long life but achieves it through selflessness."

CH'ENG CHU says, "Heaven, Earth, and Man share the same origin. Why doesn't Man share their immortality? Because Heaven and Earth are not aware they are Heaven and Earth. Only Man is aware of himself. And being aware of himself, there is nothing he won't do to stay alive. But the more he cares for his life, the more pained his life becomes. The more he nourishes his body, the sicker his body becomes. People who have not thought this out say the followers of Lao-tzu are afraid of death and only interested in immortality. But this is getting it backwards."

HO-SHANG KUNG says, "The reason Heaven and Earth alone are eternal and immortal is because they are content and give without expecting a reward, unlike Man who never stops chasing profit and fighting over possessions."

WANG PI says, "Those who live for themselves fight with others. Those who don't live for themselves are the refuge of others."

SU CH'E says, "If Heaven and Earth fought with others over life, they would be the same as others. And if the sage fought with other men over profit, he would be just another man. Would that not be a great shame?"

WANG P'ANG says, "Although the sage is a sage, he looks the same as others. But because he embodies the Way of Heaven and doesn't fight, he alone differs from everyone else. The sage is selfless because he no longer has a self."

LU TUNG-PIN says, "The only thing the sage seeks is Virtue."

8

善時。夫唯不爭。故無尤。
與善仁。言善信。政善治。事善能。動
之所惡。故幾於道。居善地。心善淵。
上善若水。水善利萬物。而不爭。處眾人

The best are like water
bringing help to all
without competing
choosing what others avoid
hence approaching the Tao
dwelling with earth
thinking with depth
helping with kindness
speaking with truth
governing with peace
working with skill
moving with time
and because they don't compete
they aren't maligned

WU CH'ENG says, "Among those who follow the Tao, the best are like water: content to be on the bottom and, thus, free of blame. Most people hate being on the bottom and compete to be on the top. And when people compete, someone is maligned."

LI HUNG-FU says, "How do we know the best don't compete? Everyone else chooses nobility. They alone choose humility. Everyone else chooses the pure. They alone choose the base. What they choose is what everyone else hates. Who is going to compete with them?"

KUAN-TZU says, "Water is the source of creation, the ancestor of all living things. It's the bloodstream of the Earth" (39).

HUANG YUAN-CHI says, "Mencius says, 'People cannot live without water and fire' (7A.23). In terms of cultivation, when fire warms water, pure *yang* arises. When water cools fire, 'sweet dew' appears."

WANG P'ANG says, "Water is the chief of the five elements (for which, see verse 12). It comes from space, which is not that far from the Tao."

WANG PI says, "The Tao does not exist, but water does. Hence it only approaches the Tao."

HO-SHANG KUNG says, "The best people have a nature like that of water. They're like mist or dew in the sky, like a stream or a spring on land. Most people hate moist or muddy places, places where water alone dwells. The nature of water is like the Tao: empty, clear, and deep. As water empties, it gives life to others. It reflects without becoming impure, and there is nothing it cannot wash clean. Water can take any shape, and it is never out of touch with the seasons. How could anyone malign something with such qualities as this."

SUNG CH'ANG-HSING says, "Those who free themselves from care stay low and avoid heights. Those whose minds are empty can plumb the depths. Those who help others without expecting any reward are truly kind. Those whose mouths agree with their minds speak the truth. Those who make demands of themselves as well as others establish peace. Those who can change as conditions change work with skill. Those who act when it is time to act and rest when it is time to rest move with time."

LI JUNG says, "Water has no purpose of its own. Those who can remain empty and not compete with others follow the natural Way."

YEN TSUN says, "If a ruler embodies this and uses this in his government, his virtue is most wonderful. How could he be maligned?"

HAN FEI says, "If a drowning man drinks it, he dies. If a thirsty man drinks it, he lives."

Given Lao-tzu's usual disdain for social virtues, some commentators have trouble accepting the standard reading of *jen:kindness* in line eight. For those in search of an alternative, the Fuyi and Chinglung editions have *jen:others*, while Mawangtui Text B has *t'ien:heaven*, and Mawangtui Text A compresses lines seven and eight: "helping with truth."

9

持而盈之。不若其已。揣而銳之。不可長保。金玉盈室。莫之能守。富貴而驕。自遺其咎。功遂身退。天之道也。

Instead of pouring in more
better stop while you can
making it sharper
won't help it last longer
houses full of treasure
can never be safe
the vanity of success
invites its own failure
when your work is done retire
this is the Way of Heaven

THE HOUHANSHU says, "What Lao-tzu warns against is 'pouring in more.'"

HSUN-TZU says, "In the ancestral hall of Duke Huan, Confucius reports watching an attendant pour water into a container that hung at an angle. As the water level approached the midpoint, the container became upright. But when the attendant went beyond the midpoint, it tipped over, the water poured out, and only after it was empty did it resume its former position. Seeing this, Confucius sighed, 'Alas! Whatever becomes full becomes empty'" (28).

LU TUNG-PIN says, "This verse is about the basics of cultivation. These are the obstacles when you first enter the gate."

LIU SHIH-LI says, "Since fullness always leads to emptiness, avoid satisfaction; since sharpness always leads to dullness, avoid zeal; since gold and jade always lead to worry, avoid greed; since wealth and honor encourage excess, avoid pride; since success and fame bring danger, know when to stop and where lies the mean. You don't have to live in the mountains and forests or cut yourself off from human affairs to enter the Way. Success and fame, wealth and honor are all encouragements to practice."

YEN TSUN says, "To succeed without being vain is easy to say but hard to practice. When success is combined with pride, it's like lighting a torch. The brighter it burns, the quicker it burns out."

WANG CHEN says, "To retire doesn't mean to abdicate your position; rather, when your task is done treat it as though it were nothing."

SSU-MA CH'IEN says, "When Confucius asked about the ceremonies of the ancients, Lao-tzu said, 'I have heard that the clever merchant hides his wealth so his store looks empty and that the superior man acts dumb to avoid calling attention to himself. I advise you to get rid of your excessive pride and ambition. They won't do you any good. This is all I have to say to you'" (63).

HO-SHANG KUNG says, "Excessive wealth and desire wearies and harms the spirit. The rich should help the poor, and the powerful should aid the oppressed. If, instead, they flaunt their riches and power, they are sure to suffer disaster. Once the sun reaches the zenith, it descends. Once the moon becomes full, it wanes. Creatures flourish then wither. Joy turns to sorrow. When your work is done, if you do not step down, you will meet with harm. This is the Way of Heaven."

HUANG YUAN-CHI says, "You need a raft to cross a river. But once across, you can forget the raft. You need to study rules to learn how to do something. But once you know how, you can forget the rules."

The Fuyi edition adds *ming-sui: when your name is made* to the beginning of line nine. The Chinglung and Chingfu editions as well as *Wentzu, Motzu,* and *Huainantzu* also include this phrase but place it after *kung-ch'eng: when your work succeeds.* Either way, its addition breaks the rhythm of the verse, which otherwise has four syllables to a line. I have treated it as an interpolation and have followed the Mawangtui texts, which condense both phrases: *kung-sui: when your work is done.*

10

載營魄抱一能無離。專氣致柔能
嬰兒。脩除玄監能無疵。愛民治
國能無為。天門開闔能為雌。明
白四達能無知。生之畜之。生而
不有。長而不宰。是謂玄德。

Can you hold fast your crescent soul and not let it wander

can you make your breath as soft as a baby's

can you wipe your Dark Mirror free of dust

can you serve and govern without effort

can you be the female at Heaven's Gate

can you light up the world without knowledge

beget things and keep them

but beget without possessing

keep without controlling

this is Dark Virtue

The Chinese say that the *hun*, or bright, ethereal, *yang* soul, governs the upper body and the *p'o*, or dark, earthly, *yin* soul, concerns itself with the lower body. Here, Lao-tzu mentions only the darker soul. But the word *p'o* also refers to the dark of the moon, and the opening phrase can also be read as referring to the first day of the new moon. Either way, dark of the soul or dark of the moon, Taoist commentators say the first line refers to the protection of our vital essence: semen and vaginal fluid, sweat and saliva, the depletion of which injures the health and leads to early death.

HSUAN-TSUNG says, "The first transformation of life is called *p'o*. When the *p'o* becomes active and bright, it is called *hun*."

WANG P'ANG says, "Life requires three things: vital essence, breath, and spirit."

CHIAO HUNG says, "The mind knows right and wrong. Breath makes no distinction. If we concentrate our breath and don't let the mind interfere with it, it remains soft and pure. Who else but a child can do this?"

CHUANG-TZU says, "The sage's mind is so still, it can mirror Heaven and Earth and reflect the ten thousand things" (13.1).

WU CH'ENG says, "Our spirit dwells in our eyes. When the eyes see something, the spirit chases it. When we close our eyes and look within, everything is dark. But within the dark, we still see something. There is still dust. Only by putting an end to delusions can we get rid of the dust."

WANG AN-SHIH says, "The best way to serve is by not serving. The best way to govern is by not governing. Hence Lao-tzu says 'without effort.' Those who act without effort make use of the efforts of others. As for Heaven's Gate, this is the gate through which all creatures enter and leave. To be open means to be active. To be closed means to be still. Activity and stillness represent the male and the female. Just as stillness overcomes movement, the female overcomes the male."

SU CH'E says, "What lights up the world is the mind. There is nothing the mind does not know. And yet no none can know the mind. The mind is one. If someone knew it, there would be two. Going from one to two is the origin of all delusion."

LAO-TZU says, "The Tao begets them / Virtue keeps them" (51).

WANG PI says, "If we don't obstruct their source, things come into existence on their own. If we don't suppress their nature, things mature by themselves. Virtue is present, but its owner is unknown. It comes from the mysterious depths. Hence we call it dark."

The first line has had numerous interpretations, to which I have added one more. CHENG LIANG-SHU and most other modern commentators now agree that *tsai* should be placed at the beginning of this verse instead of at the end of the previous verse. Although *tsai* can mean "carry," it can also mean "new," as in the phrase: *tsai-sheng-p'o:new-born moon,* or as Lao-tzu uses it here: *tsai-ying-p'o:new-lit moon/soul.* After line eight, most editions add "act without presuming," which also appears in a similar sequence in verses 2 and 51. I have followed the Mawangtui texts in omitting it here as irrelevant.

11

卅輻共一轂。當其無。有車之用。挺埴以為器。當其無。有器之用。鑿戶牖以為室。當其無。有室之用。故有之以為利。無之以為用。

Thirty spokes converge on a hub
but it's the emptiness
that makes a wheel work
pots are fashioned from clay
but it's the hollow
that makes a pot work
windows and doors are carved for a house
but it's the spaces
that make a house work
existence makes something useful
but nonexistence makes it work

HSUAN-TSUNG says, "Thirty spokes converging on a hub demonstrates that less is the ancestor of more."

HO-SHANG KUNG says, "Ancient carts had thirty spokes in imitation of the lunar number."

LI-JUNG says, "It's because the hub is empty that spokes converge on it. Likewise, it's because the sage's mind is empty that the people turn to him for help."

CH'ENG HSUAN-YING says, "A cart, a pot, and a house can hold things because they are empty. How much more the disciple who empties his mind."

WU CH'ENG says, "All of these things are useful. But without an empty place for an axle, a cart can't move. Without a hollow place in the middle, a pot can't hold things. Without spaces for doors and windows, a room can't admit people or light. But these three examples are only metaphors. What keeps our body alive is the existence of breath in our stomach. And it is our empty, nonexistent mind that produces breath."

SUNG CH'ANG-HSING says, "In this verse the Great Sage teaches us to understand the source by using what we find at hand. Doors refer to a person's mouth and nose. Windows refer to their ears and eyes."

CHANG TAO-LING says, "When ordinary people see these things, they only think about how they might employ them for their own advantage. When the sage sees them, he sees in them the Tao and is careful in their use."

TE-CH'ING says. "Heaven and Earth have form, and everyone knows that Heaven and Earth are useful. But they don't know that their usefulness depends on the emptiness of the Great Way. Likewise, we all have form and think ourselves useful but remain unaware that our usefulness depends on our empty, shapeless mind. Thus existence may have its uses, but real usefulness depends on nonexistence. Nonexistence, though, doesn't work by itself. It needs the help of existence."

HUANG YUAN-CHI says, "What is beyond form is the Tao, while what has form are tools. Without tools we have no means to apprehend the Tao. And without the Tao there is no place for tools."

HSUEH HUI says, "At the end of this verse, Lao-tzu mentions both existence and nonexistence, but his intent is to use existence to show that nonexistence is more valuable. Everyone knows existence is useful, but no one pays attention to the usefulness of nonexistence."

In line seven, the Mawangtui texts omit yi-wei-shih:for a house, but this phrase is needed to complete the line and is present in all other editions. Many people in Shensi and Honan provinces still carve their homes into the loess cliffs that distinguish this region where Chinese civilization first developed and where this text was written. The compactness of the soil makes support beams unnecessary, and its density keeps dwellings cool in the summer and warm in the winter. The only building materials needed are doors and windows.

12

五色使人目盲。五音使人耳聾。五味使人口爽。馳騁田獵使人心發狂。難得之貨使人行妨。是以聖人之治。為腹而不為目。故去彼而取此。

The five colors make our eyes blind
the five tones make our ears deaf
the five flavors make our mouths numb
riding and hunting make our minds wild
hard-to-get goods make us break laws
thus the rule of the sage
puts the stomach ahead of the eyes
thus he picks this over that

The early Chinese ascribed five states of existence to the material world: water, fire, wood, metal, and earth—each with its own color: blue, red, black, white, and yellow; its own taste: salty, bitter, sour, pungent, and sweet; and its own tone: la, sol, mi, re, do.

YEN TSUN says, "Color is like an awl in the eye. Sound is like a stick in the ear. Flavor is like an axe through the tongue."

TE-CH'ING says, "When the eyes are given free rein in the realm of form, they no longer see what is real. When the ears are given free rein the realm of sound, they no longer hear what is real. When the tongue is given free rein in the realm of taste, it no longer discerns what is real. When the mind is given free rein in the realm of thought, it no longer knows what is real. When our actions are given free rein in the realm of possession and profit, we no longer do what is right. Like Chuang-tzu's tapir (1.4), the sage drinks from the river, but only enough to fill his stomach.

WU CH'ENG says, "Desiring external things harms our bodies. The sage nourishes his breath by filling his stomach, not by chasing material objects to please his eye. Hence he chooses internal reality over external illusion. But the eyes can't help seeing, the ears can't help hearing, the mouth can't help tasting, the mind can't help feeling, and the body can't help moving. They can't stay still. But if we let them move without leaving stillness behind, nothing can harm us. Those who are buried by the dust of the senses or who crave sensory stimulation lose their way. And the main villain in this is the eyes. Thus the first of Confucius' four warnings concerns vision (Lunyu: 12.1: not to look except with propriety), and the first of the Buddha's six sources of delusion is also the eyes."

LI YUEH says, "The eyes are never satisfied, the stomach knows when it is full."

SUNG CH'ANG-HSING says, "The main purpose of cultivation is to oppose the world of the senses. What the world loves, the Taoist hates. What the world wants, the Taoist rejects. Even though color, sound, material goods, wealth, or beauty might benefit a person's body, in the end they harm a person's mind. And once the mind wants, the body suffers. If we can ignore external temptations and be satisfied with the way we are, if we can cultivate our mind and not chase material things, this is the way of long life. All the treasures of the world are no match for this."

HSUAN-TSUNG says, "'Hard-to-get goods' refer to things which we don't possess by nature but which require an effort to obtain. When we are not content with our lot and allow ourselves to be ruled by conceit, we turn our backs on Heaven and lose the Way."

CH'ENG HSUAN-YING says, "'That' refers to the blindness and delusion of the eyes. 'This' refers to the fullness and wisdom of the stomach."

The Mawangtui texts present lines two through five in a different sequence: 4, 5, 3, 2. However, no other edition follows suit, hence I have retained the traditional order. Until the early twentieth century, vast tracts of land in northern China were set aside for the exclusive use of the nobility and the military in conducting group hunts to practice their riding and archery.

13

天下。若可以寄天下。

何患。故貴以身為天下。若可以託天下。愛以身為

若身。吾所以有大患者。為吾有身。及吾無身。有

得之若驚。失之若驚。是謂寵辱若驚。何謂貴大患

寵辱若驚。貴大患若身。何謂寵辱若驚。寵之為下。

Favor and disgrace are like warnings
honor and disaster are like the body
and why are favor and disgrace like warnings
favor means descending
to gain it is like a warning
to lose it is like a warning
thus are favor and disgrace like warnings
and why are honor and disaster like the body
the reason we have disaster
is because we have a body
if we didn't have a body
we wouldn't have disaster
who honors his body as much as the world
can be entrusted with the world
who loves his body as much as the world
can be encharged with the world

WANG CHEN says, "People who are favored are honored. And because they are honored, they act proud. And because they act proud, they are hated. And because they are hated, they are disgraced. Hence the sage considers success as well as failure to be a warning."

SU CH'E says, "The ancient sages worried about favor as much as disgrace, because they knew that favor is followed by disgrace. Other people think favor means to go up, and disgrace means to go down. But favor cannot be separated from disgrace. Disgrace comes from favor."

HO-SHANG KUNG says, "Those who gain favor or honor should worry about being too high, as if they were at the edge of a precipice. They should not flaunt their status or wealth. And those who lose favor and live in disgrace should worry about another disaster."

LU NUNG-SHIH says, "Why does favor become disgrace and honor become disaster? Favor and honor are external things. They don't belong to us. When we try to possess them, they turn into disgrace and disaster."

SSU-MA KUANG says, "Normally a body means disaster. But if we honor and cherish it and follow the natural order in our dealings with others and don't indulge our desires, we can avoid disaster."

HUANG YUAN-CHI says, "We all possess something good and noble that we don't have to seek outside ourselves, something that the glory of power or position cannot compare with. People need only start with this and cultivate without letting up. The ancients said, 'Two or three years of hardship, ten thousand years of bliss.'"

WANG P'ANG says, "It isn't a matter of having no body but of guarding the source of life. Someone who refuses to trade himself for something external is fit to receive the kingdom."

WANG PI says, "Those who are affected by favor or disgrace, honor or disaster are not fit to receive the kingdom."

TSENG-TZU says, "The superior man can be entrusted with an orphan or encharged with a state and be unmoved by a crisis" (*Lunyu*: 8.6).

Commentators disagree about how to read line one: is "favor" a verb and "disgrace" its noun object ("favor disgrace as a warning") or are they both nouns? The same question is posed for "honor" and "disaster" in line two. Some editions omit *juo-ching:like warnings* in line three and have two quite different lines for line four: "favor means up / disgrace means down." My choice is based on the Fuyi and Mawangtui texts, as well as Wang Pi. The last four lines are also found in *Chuangtzu:* 11.2, where they are used to praise the ruler whose self-cultivation doesn't leave him time to meddle in the lives of his subjects. They also appear in *Huainantzu:* 12, where they are used to praise the ruler who values the lives of his people more than the territory in which they live.

14

視之不見。名曰夷。聽之不聞。名曰希。搏之不得。名曰微。三者
不可致詰。故混而為一。其上不皦。在下不昧。繩繩兮不可名。復
歸於無物。是謂無狀之狀。無物之象。是謂忽恍。迎而不見其首
。隨而不見其後。執今之道。以御今之有。以知古始。是謂道紀。

We look but don't see it
and call it indistinct
we listen but don't hear it
and call it faint
we reach but don't grasp it
and call it ethereal
three failed means to knowledge
we weave into one
with no light above
with no shade below
too fine to be named
returning to nothing
this is the formless form
the immaterial image
this is the waxing waning
we meet without seeing its face
we follow without seeing its back
holding onto this very Way
we rule this very realm
and discover its ancient past
this is the thread of the Way

HO-SHANG KUNG entitles this verse "In Praise of the Dark" and says, "About what has no color, sound, or form, mouths can't speak and books can't teach. We can only discover it in stillness and search for it with our spirit. We can't find it through investigation."

LU TUNG-PIN says, "We can only see it inside us, hear it inside us, and grasp it inside us. When our essence becomes one, we can see it. When our breath becomes one, we can hear it. When our spirit becomes one, we can grasp it."

CH'ENG HSUAN-YING says, "What we don't see is vital essence. What we don't hear is spirit. What we don't grasp is breath."

SU CH'E says, "People see things constantly changing and conclude something is there. They don't realize everything returns to nothing."

CH'EN KU-YING says, "Nothing doesn't mean nothing at all but simply no form or substance."

WANG PI says, "If we try to claim it doesn't exist, how do the myriad things come to be? And if we try to claim it exists, why don't we see its form? Hence we call it the formless form. But although it has neither shape nor form, neither sound nor echo, there is nothing it cannot penetrate and nowhere it cannot go."

LI YUEH says, "Everything is bright on top and dark on the bottom. But the Tao does not have a top or bottom. Hence it is neither bright nor dark. Likewise, we do not see its face because it never appears, and we do not see its back because it never leaves."

TS'AO TAO-CH'UNG says, "'This very realm' refers to our body."

LU HUI-CH'ING says, "The past isn't different from today, because we know what began in the past. And today isn't different from the past, because we know where today came from. What neither begins nor comes from anywhere else we call the thread that has no end. This is the thread of the Tao."

CHANG TAO-LING says, "The sages who achieved long life and immortality in the past all succeeded by means of this Tao. Who can follow their example today has found the thread of the Tao."

In line eight, I have extended the thread motif by going along with Mawangtui Text B in reading *chun:weave* instead of the usual *hun:merge.* I have also chosen the Mawangtui versions of lines fifteen and eighteen, which the standard edition renders: "this is the indefinable" and "holding onto the ancient Tao."

15

古之善為道者。微眇。玄通。深不可識。夫唯不可識。故強
為之容。曰與兮其若冬涉川。猶兮其若畏四鄰。嚴兮其若客
。渙兮其若凌釋。敦兮其若朴。曠兮其若浴。混兮其若濁
。濁而靜之徐清。安以動之徐生。保此道不欲盈。夫唯不
欲盈。是以能蔽而不成。

The ancient masters of the Way
aimed at the indiscernible
and penetrated the dark
you would never know them
and because you wouldn't know them
I describe them with reluctance
they were careful as if crossing a river in winter
cautious as if worried about neighbors
reserved like guests
ephemeral like melting ice
simple like uncarved wood
open like valleys
and murky like puddles
but a puddle becomes clear when it's still
and stillness becomes alive when it's roused
those who treasure this Way
don't try to be full
not trying to be full
they can hide and stay hidden

TS'AO TAO-CH'UNG says, "Although the ancient masters lived in the world, no one thought they were special."

SU CH'E says, "Darkness is what penetrates everything but cannot itself be perceived. To be careful means to act only after taking precautions. To be cautious means to refrain from acting because of doubt or suspicion. Melting ice reminds us how the myriad things arise from delusion and never stay still. Uncarved wood reminds us to put an end to human fabrication and return to our original nature. A valley reminds us how encompassing emptiness is. And a puddle reminds us that we are no different from anything else."

HUANG YUAN-CHI says, "Lao-tzu expresses reluctance at describing those who succeed in cultivating the Tao because he knows the inner truth cannot be perceived, only the outward form. The essence of the Tao consists in nothing other than taking care. If people took care to let each thought be detached and each action well-considered, where else would they find the Tao? Hence those who mastered the Tao in the past were so careful they waited until a river froze before crossing. They were so cautious, they waited until the wind died down before venturing forth at night. They were orderly and respectful, as if they were guests arriving from a distant land. They were relaxed and detached, as if material forms didn't matter. They were as uncomplicated as uncarved wood and as hard to fathom as murky water. They stilled themselves to concentrate their spirit and roused themselves to strengthen their breath. In short, they guarded the center."

WANG PI says, "All of these similes are meant to describe without actually denoting. By means of intuitive understanding the dark becomes bright. By means of tranquility, the murky becomes clear. By means of movement, the still becomes alive. This is the natural Way."

HO-SHANG KUNG says, "Those who aren't full are able to maintain their concealment and avoid new attainments."

WANG CHEN says, "Those who can keep to the Way fit in without making a show and stay forever hidden. Hence they don't leave any tracks."

In line two, I have used Mawangtui Text B in reading *miao:aim* for *miao: mysterious*. Other variants of the last line include: "they can be old but not new" and "they can be old and again new." My reading is based on the Fuyi edition and Mawangtui Text B as well as on the interpretation of Wang Pi and Ho-shang Kung, who read *pi:hide* instead of *pi:old,* thus recapitulating the opening lines.

16

至虛極。守靜篤。萬物並作。吾以觀其復。夫物紜紜。各

復歸其根。歸根曰靜。靜曰復命。復命曰常。知常曰明。

不知常妄作凶。知常容。容乃公。公乃王。王乃天。天

乃道。道乃久。沒身不殆。

Let limits be empty

the center be still

ten thousand things rise

we watch them return

creatures without number

all return to their roots

return to their roots to be still

to be still to revive

to revive to endure

knowing how to endure is wisdom

not knowing is to suffer in vain

knowing how to endure is to be all-embracing

all-embracing means impartial

impartial means the king

the king means Heaven

Heaven means the Way

and the Way means long life

life without trouble

SUNG CH'ANG-HSING says, "Emptiness is the Way of Heaven. Stillness is the way of Earth. There is nothing that is not endowed with these, and everything rises by means of them."

LU HUI-CH'ING says, "What is meant here by emptiness is not total emptiness but the absence of fullness. And what is meant by stillness is not complete stillness but everything unconsciously returning to its roots."

HUANG YUAN-CHI says, "Heaven has its fulcrum, people have their ancestors, plants have their roots. And where are these roots? Where things begin but have not yet begun, namely, the Dark Gate. If you want to cultivate the Great Way, but you don't know where this opening is, your efforts will be in vain."

SU CH'E says, "We all rise from our nature and return to our nature, just as flowers and leaves rise from their roots and return to their roots, or just as waves rise from water and return to water. If you don't return to your nature, even if you still your actions and thoughts, you won't be still. Heaven and Earth, mountains and rivers might be great, but none of them endures. Only what returns to its nature becomes still and enduring, while what does not return to its nature is at the mercy of others and cannot escape."

CH'ENG HSUAN-YING says, "He who embraces all things and is impartial and selfless becomes a great example to others who thus turn to him as their ruler."

TE-CH'ING says, "To know what truly endures is to know that Heaven and Earth share the same root, that the ten thousand things share one body, and that there is no difference between self and others. Those who cultivate this within themselves become sages, while those who practice this in the world become rulers. Rulers become rulers by following the Way of Heaven. And Heaven becomes Heaven by following the Tao. And the Tao becomes the Tao by lasting forever."

HO-SHANG KUNG says, "To know the unchanging course of the Way is to be free of passion and desire and to be all-embracing. To be all-embracing is to be free of self-interest. To be free of self-interest is to rule the world. To rule the world is to merge your virtue with that of Heaven. And to merge your virtue with that of Heaven is to be one with the Way. If you can do this, you will last as long as Heaven and Earth and live without trouble."

LI JUNG says, "The sage enjoys a life without limits."

My reading of line two is based on Cheng Liang-shu's interpretation of Mawangtui Text B, which has *tu:center* in place of the usual *tu:true*. The last line also appears in verse 52.

17

太上下知有之。其次親譽
之。其次畏之。其次侮之。
信不足。安有不信。猶兮
其貴言也。成功遂事。而
百姓謂我自然。

During the High Ages people knew they were there
then people loved and praised them
then they feared them
finally they despised them
when honesty fails
dishonesty prevails
hesitate and guard your words
when their work succeeds
let people think they did it

The Chinese of Lao-tzu's day believed their greatest age of peace and harmony occurred during the reigns of the Three Sovereigns and Five Emperors, or nearly five thousand years ago. These early rulers exercised power so unobtrusively, the people hardly knew they were there, as we hear in a song handed down from that distant age: "Sunup we rise / sundown we rest / we dig wells to drink / we plough fields to eat / the emperor's might / what is it to us?" (*Kushihyuan: 1*).

THE LICHI says, "During the High Ages people esteemed virtue. Then they worked for rewards" (1).

LU HSI-SHENG says, "The virtuous lords of ancient times initiated no actions and left no traces, hence the people knew they were there and that was all. When their virtue began to fade, they ruled with kindness and justice, and the people loved and praised them. When their kindness and justice no longer controlled people's hearts, they governed with laws and punishments, and the people feared them. When their laws and punishments no longer controlled people's minds, they acted with force and deceit, and the people despised them."

MENCIUS says, "When the ruler views his ministers as his hands and feet, they regard him as their heart and soul. When he views them as dirt and weeds, they regard him as an enemy and thief" (4B.3).

SUNG CH'ANG-HSING says, "The mistake of loving and praising, fearing and despising does not rest with the people but with those above. The reason the people turn to love and praise, fear and hate is because those above cannot be trusted. And when trust disappears, chaos appears."

HUANG YUAN-CHI says, "What we do to cultivate ourselves is what we do to govern the world. And among the arts we cultivate, the most subtle of all is honesty, which is the beginning and end of cultivation. When we embrace the truth, the world enjoys peace. When we turn our backs on the truth, the world suffers. From the time of the Three Sovereigns and Five Emperors, this has never varied."

HO-SHANG KUNG says, "When those above treat those below with dishonesty, those below respond with deceit."

WANG PI says, "Where there are words, there is a response. Thus the sage hesitates."

WU CH'ENG says, "The reason sages don't speak or act is so that they can bestow their blessings in secret and so that people can live their lives in peace. And when their work succeeds and their lives go well, people think that is just the way it is supposed to be. They don't realize it was made possible by those on high."

LU HUI-CH'ING says, "As long as the people think they did it themselves, they have no reason to love or praise anyone."

In line one, some editions have *pu-chih:did not know* in place of *hsia-chih:people knew.* I have chosen the latter version, as have the Mawangtui and Fuyi texts. The Fuyi text divides line two into two lines: "then they loved them / then they praised them." Despite the attractiveness of such a variation, placing *ch'in:love* in a separate line interrupts the rhyme. Also, some commentators combine this verse with the following two verses, citing a similarity in theme. However, the wide variation among their rhythms argues against this.

18

大道廢。安有仁義。六

智慧出。安有大偽。邦

親不和。安有孝慈。

家昏亂。安有貞臣。

When the Great Way disappears
we meet kindness and justice
when reason appears
we meet great deceit
when the six relations fail
we meet obedience and love
when the country is in chaos
we meet honest officials

Connecting this with the previous verse, WEI YUAN says, "What people love and praise are kindness and justice, what people fear is reason, and what people despise is deceit."

SUNG CH'ANG-HSING says, "It isn't the Great Way that leaves mankind and goes into hiding, but mankind that leaves the Great Way and replaces it with kindness and justice."

SU CH'E says, "When the Great Way flourishes, kindness and justice are at work, but people don't realize it. Only after the Great Way disappears do kindness and justice become visible."

WANG AN-SHIH says, "The Way hides in formlessness. Names arise from discontent. When the Way hides in formlessness, there isn't any difference between great or small. When names arise from discontent, we get distinctions like kindness, justice, reason, and so forth."

HO-SHANG KUNG says, "When the kingdom enjoys peace, no one thinks about kindness, and the people are free of desire. When the Great Way prevails, kindness and justice vanish, just as the stars fade when the sun rises."

MENCIUS says, "Kindness means dwelling in peace. Justice means taking the right road" (4A.10).

TE-CH'ING says, "Reason is what the sage uses to order the kingdom. It includes the arts, measurements, and laws. In the High Ages, people were innocent, and these were unknown. In the Middle Ages, people began to indulge their feelings, and rulers responded with reason. And once reason appeared, the people responded with deceit."

WANG PI says, "The six relations are father and son, elder and younger brother, husband and wife. When the six relations are harmonious, the country governs itself, and there is no need for obedience, love, or honesty."

WANG P'ANG says, "During a virtuous age, obedience and love are considered normal, hence no one is called obedient or loving. Nowadays, when someone is obedient or loving, we praise them. This is because the six relations are no longer harmonious. Also, when peace prevails, everyone is honest. How can there be honest officials?"

CH'ENG HSUAN-YING says, "When the realm is at peace, loyalty and honesty are nowhere to be seen. Innocence and virtue appear when the realm is in chaos."

LI JUNG says, "During the time of the sage emperors Fu Hsi and Shen Nung, there was no mention of officials. It was only during the time of the despots Chieh and Chou that we begin to hear of ministers like Kuan Lung-feng and Pi Kan."

WU CH'ENG says, "Shao Juo-yu assigns these four divisions to emperors, kings, the wise, and the talented."

Both Mawangtui texts begin this verse with the word ku:thus, implying a connection with the previous verse. I think it does better on its own, hence I have followed the Fuyi and standard editions, which have no such connective. Commentators often quote *Chuangtzu* here: "When springs dry up, fish find themselves in puddles, spraying water on each other to keep each other alive. Better to be in a river or lake and oblivious of each other" (6.5).

19

絕聖棄知。民利百倍。絕仁棄義。
民復孝慈。絕巧棄利。盜賊無有。
此三言以為文未足。故令之有所
屬。見素抱朴。少私寡欲。絕學無
憂。

Get rid of wisdom and reason
and people will live a hundred times better
get rid of kindness and justice
and people once more will love and obey
get rid of cleverness and profit
and thieves will cease to exist
but these three sayings are not enough
hence let this be added
wear the undyed and hold the uncarved
reduce self-interest and limit desires
get rid of learning and problems will vanish

HO-SHANG KUNG says, "Get rid of the works of wisdom and reason and return to the primeval. The symbols and letters created by the Five Emperors were not as effective in ruling the kingdom as the simple knots used earlier by the Three Sovereigns."

TE-CH'ING says, "This is what Chuang-tzu meant when he said 'Tigers and wolves are kind.' Tigers and wolves possess innate love and obedience that don't require instruction. How much more should mankind, the most intelligent of creatures, possess these."

WANG CHEN says, "Put an end to wisdom that leaves tracks and reason that deceives, and people will benefit greatly. Put an end to arrogant kindness and treacherous justice, and relatives will unite on their own and will once more love and obey. Put an end to excessive cleverness and personal profit, and armies will no longer appear. And when armies no longer appear, thieves will not exist."

HSUAN-TSUNG says, "These three only help us get rid of things. They don't explain cultivation. Hence they are incomplete."

WANG PI says, "Wisdom and reason are the pinnacles of ability. Kindness and justice are the pinnacles of behavior. Cleverness and profit are the pinnacles of practice. To tell us simply to get rid of them would be inappropriate. Without giving us something else, it wouldn't make sense. Hence we are given the undyed and the uncarved to focus our attention on."

CHIAO HUNG says, "The ways of the world become daily more artificial. Hence we have names like wisdom and reason, kindness and justice, cleverness and profit. Those who understand the Tao see how artificial they are and how inappropriate they are to rule the world. They aren't as good as getting people to focus their attention on the undyed and the uncarved. By wearing the undyed and holding the uncarved, our self-interest and desires wane. The undyed and the uncarved refer to our original nature."

LIU CHING says, "Undyed means unmixed with anything else and thus free of wisdom and reason. Uncarved means complete in itself and thus free of kindness and justice. Self-interest concerns oneself. Desire concerns others. As they diminish, so do cleverness and profit."

SU CH'E says, "Confucius relied on kindness and justice, ritual and music to order the kingdom. Lao-tzu's only concern was to open people's minds, which he accomplished through the use of metaphor. Some people, though, have used his metaphors to create disorder, while no great problems have been caused by the followers of Confucius."

CH'ENG HSUAN-YING says, "When we give up the study of phenomena and understand the principle of non-interference, troubles come to an end and distress disappears."

LI HSI-CHAI says, "What passes for learning in the world never ends. For every truth found, two are lost. And while what we find brings joy, losses bring sorrow—sorrow that never ends."

I have followed Kao Heng in moving the line that normally begins the next verse to the end of this verse, where it makes better sense as well as better poetry.

20

Yes and no
aren't so far apart
lovely and ugly
aren't so unalike
what others fear
we too must fear
before the moon wanes
everyone is gay
as if they were at the Great Sacrifice
or climbing a tower in spring
I sit here and make no sign
like a child that doesn't smile
lost with no one to turn to
while others enjoy more
I alone seem forgotten
my mind is so foolish
so simple
others look bright
I alone seem dim
others are certain
I alone am confused
receding like the ocean
waxing without cease
everyone has a goal
I alone am dumb and backward
for I alone choose to differ
preferring still my mother's breast

唯與訶。其相去幾何。美與惡。其相去何若。人之所畏。亦不可不畏。望兮其未央哉。眾人熙熙。若饗於大牢。而春登臺。我泊焉未兆。若嬰兒未咳。累兮若無所歸。眾人皆有餘。我獨若遺。我愚人之心也。純純兮。俗人昭昭。我獨若昏兮。俗人察察。我獨湣湣兮。泅兮其若海。望兮其若無所止。眾人皆有以。我獨頑且鄙。我獨欲異於人。而貴食母。

CH'ENG HSUAN-YING says, *Wei:yes* indicates agreement and *k'o:no* disdain.

SUNG CH'ANG-HSING says, "Even though "yes" and "no" come from the same source, namely the mouth, "yes" is the root of loveliness, and "no" is the root of ugliness. Before they appear there is nothing lovely or ugly and nothing to fear. But once they appear, if we don't fear them, disaster and harm are unavoidable."

LI HSI-CHAI says, "What others love, the sage also loves. What others fear, the sage also fears. But where the sage differs is where others don't see anything outside their own minds. The mind of the sage, meanwhile, wanders in the Tao."

WANG P'ANG says, "Everything changes into its opposite. Beginning follows end without cease. But people think everything is either lovely or ugly. How absurd. Only the sage knows that the ten thousand ages are the same, that nothing is gained or lost."

SU CH'E says, "People all drown in what they love: the beauty of the Great Sacrifice, the happiness of climbing to a scenic viewpoint in spring. Only the sage sees into their illusory nature and remains unmoved. People chase things and forget about the Tao, while the sage clings to the Tao and ignores everything else, just as an infant nurses only at its mother's breast."

TS'AO TAO-CH'UNG says, "People all seek external things, while the sage alone nourishes himself on internal breath. Breath is the mother, and spirit is the child. The harmony of mother and child is the key to nourishing life."

In ancient China, emperors marked the return of swallows to the capital in spring with the Great Sacrifice to the Supreme Intermediary, while people of all ranks climbed towers and hills to view the countryside in bloom and to celebrate the first full moon. In line seven, I have followed Mawangtui Text B in reading *wang:full moon* instead of the usual *huang:boundless*. I have used the same variant in line twenty-three.

21

以順眾父。吾何以知眾父之然也。以此。

精兮。其精甚真。其中有信。自今及古。其名不去。

兮。中有象兮。恍兮惚兮。中有物兮。窈兮冥兮。中有

孔德之容。唯道是從。道之為物。唯恍唯惚。惚兮恍

The expression of empty virtue

comes from the Tao alone

the Tao as a thing

waxes and wanes

it waxes and wanes

but inside there is an image

it wanes and waxes

but inside there is a creature

it's distant and dark

but inside there is an essence

an essence fundamentally real

and inside there is a heart

throughout the ages

its name has never changed

so we might follow our fathers

how do we know what our fathers were like

through this

WANG PI says, "Only when we take emptiness as our virtue can our actions accord with the Tao."

SUNG CH'ANG-HSING says, "Sages have it. So does everyone else. But because others are selfish and constrained, their virtue isn't empty."

HUANG YUAN-CHI says, "Emptiness and the Tao are indivisible. Those who seek the Tao cannot find it except through emptiness. But formless emptiness is of no use to those who cultivate the Tao."

YEN LING-FENG says, "Virtue is the manifestation of the Way. The Way is what Virtue contains. Without the Way, Virtue would have no power. Without Virtue, the Way would have no appearance."

SU CH'E says, "The Tao has no form. Only when it changes into Virtue does it have an expression. Hence Virtue is the Tao's visual aspect. The Tao neither exists nor does not exist. Hence we say it waxes and wanes, while it remains in the dark unseen."

CH'ENG HSUAN-YING says, "The true Tao exists and yet does not exist. It does not exist and yet does not not exist. Lao-tzu says it waxes and wanes to stress that the Tao is not separate from things and things are not separate from the Tao. Outside of the Tao there are no things. And outside of things there is no Tao."

WU CH'ENG says, "'Inside' refers to Virtue. 'Image' refers to the breath of something before it is born. 'Creature' refers to the form of something after it is born. 'Distant and dark' refers to the utter invisibility of the Tao."

CHANG TAO-LING says, "Essence is like water: the body is its embankment, and Virtue is its source. If the heart is not virtuous, or if there is no embankment, water disappears. The immortals of the past treasured their essence and lived, while people today lose their essence and die."

WANG P'ANG says, "Essence is where life and the body come from. Lao-tzu calls it 'fundamentally real' because once things become subject to human fabrication, they lose their reality."

LIU CHING says, "Everything changes, and names are no exception. What was true in the past is false today. Only the Tao is constant."

The Mawangtui texts have introduced a number of new variants into this verse. Those which I have incorporated include *wang:full moon* for *huang: indistinct* in lines four, five, and seven; *shun:follow* for *yueh:view* and *fu:father* for *fu:beginning* in line fifteen. The standard version of fifteen and sixteen reads: "so we might view all beginnings / and how do we know what all beginnings are like." Also, in line twelve, I have read *hsin:lamp wick* (and hence the heart of something) in place of the word's usual meaning as "talisman" (and hence something trustworthy).

22

曲則全。枉則正。窪則盈。弊則新。少則得。多則惑。是以聖人執一。以為天下牧。不自視故明。不自見故章。不自伐故有功。不自矜故能長。夫唯不爭。故莫能與之爭。古之所謂曲則全者。幾語哉。成全歸之。

Partial means whole

crooked means straight

hollow means full

worn-out means new

less means content

more means confused

thus the sage holds onto the one

to use in guiding the world

not watching himself he appears

not displaying himself he flourishes

not flattering himself he succeeds

not parading himself he leads

because he doesn't compete

no one can compete against him

the ancients who said partial means whole

came close indeed

becoming whole depends on this

CHUANG-TZU says, "Lao-tzu said everyone else seeks happiness. He alone saw that partial means whole" (33.5).

WU CH'ENG says, "By exploring one side to its limits, we eventually find all sides. By grasping one thing, we eventually encompass the whole. The caterpillar bends in order to straighten itself. A hollow in the ground fills with water. The renewal of spring depends on the withering of fall. By having less, it's easy to have more. By having more, it's easy to become confused."

WANG PI says, "As with a tree, the more of it there is, the farther it is from its roots. The less of it there is, the closer it is to its roots. More means more distant from what is real. Less means closer."

WEI YUAN says, "One is the extreme of less. But whoever uses this as the measure for the world always finds more."

LU HUI-CH'ING says, "Only those who find the one can act like this. Thus 'less means content.' The reason most people cannot act like this is because they have not found the one. Thus 'more means confused.'"

LI HSI-CHAI says, "The reason the sage is able to be chief of all creatures is because he holds onto the one. Holding onto the one, he never leaves the Tao. Hence he doesn't watch himself but relies instead on the vision of others. He doesn't talk about his own strengths but relies instead on the strengths of others. He stands apart and doesn't compete. Hence no one can compete against him."

HSUAN-TSUNG says, "Not watching himself, he becomes whole. Not displaying himself, he becomes straight. Not flattering himself, he becomes full. Not parading himself, he becomes new."

TZU-SSU says, "Only those who are perfectly honest can fulfill their nature and help others fulfill their nature. Next are those who are partial" (*Chungyung*: 22–23).

MENCIUS says, "We praise those who don't calculate. We reproach those who try to be whole" (4A.21).

HO-SHANG KUNG says, "Those who are able to practice being partial keep their physical body whole. Those who depend on their mother and father suffer no harm."

For the wording of lines eight through thirteen as well as line sixteen, I have followed the Mawangtui texts. Lines nine through twelve appear in slightly different form in verse 24. In the last line, my use of *ch'eng:become* in place of the usual *ch'eng:honest* is based on Tunhuang texts s.6453 and p.2584, the Suichou and Chinglung editions, and on Chu Ch'ien-chih's observation that *ch'eng:honest* appears nowhere else in the *Taoteching*, while *ch'eng:become* occurs seventeen times. The interpolation of "honest" was apparently influenced by the passage from Tzu-ssu's *Chungyung* quoted above.

23

希言自然。飄風不終朝。暴雨不終日。孰為此

天地。天地而不能久。況於人乎。故從事。而道

者同於道。得者同於得。失者同於失。同於得

者。道亦得之。同於失者。道亦失之。

Whispered words are natural
a gale doesn't last all morning
a squall doesn't last all day
who else could make these
only Heaven and Earth
if Heaven and Earth can't make things last
what about Man
thus in whatever we do
let those on the Way be one with the Way
let those who succeed be one with success
let those who fail be one with failure
be one with success
for the Way succeeds too
be one with failure
for the Way fails too

WU CH'ENG says, "'Whispered' means not heard. 'Whispered words' means no words. Those who reach the Tao forget about words and follow whatever is natural."

WANG CHEN says, "Whispered words require less effort. Hence they conform to the natural Way."

LU NUNG-SHIH says, "Something is natural when nothing can make it so, and nothing can make it not so."

CH'ENG HSUAN-YING says, "If the greatest forces wrought by Heaven and Earth cannot last, how can the works of Man?"

SU CH'E says, "The sage's words are faint, and his deeds are plain. But they are always natural. Hence he can last and not be exhausted."

TE-CH'ING says, "This verse explains how the sage forgets about words, embodies the Tao, and changes with the seasons. Elsewhere, Lao-tzu says, 'talking only wastes it / better to keep it inside' (5). Those who love to argue get farther from the Way. They aren't natural. Only those whose words are whispered are natural. Lao-tzu uses wind and rain storms as metaphors for the outbursts of those who love to argue. They can't maintain such a disturbance and dissipation of breath very long. Because they don't really believe in the Tao, their actions don't accord with the Tao. They haven't learned the secret of how to be one."

CHIAO HUNG says, "Those who pursue the Way are natural. Natural means free from success and hence free from failure. Such people don't succeed and don't fail but simply go along with the successes and failures of the age. Or if they do succeed or fail, their minds are not affected."

LU HUI-CH'ING says, "Those who pursue the Way are able to leave their selves behind. No self is the Way. Success. Failure. I don't see how they differ."

HO-SHANG KUNG says, "Those who are one with success enjoy succeeding. Those who are one with failure enjoy failing. Water is wet, and fire burns. This is their nature."

Many commentators have noted that the latter half of the standard version of this verse is marked by an awkward use of rhythm and rhyme, and most have found it confusing. I have used the simpler and smoother Mawangtui version. However, in lines ten, twelve, and thirteen, I have chosen the Fuyi text, which has *te:succeed* in place of the usual *te:virtue*. Both characters were interchangeable when this text was composed, and "virtue" is clearly out of place here. The standard and Fuyi versions add this couplet to the end of the verse: "where honesty fails / dishonesty prevails." These lines also appear in verse 17. However, they are not present in either of the Mawangtui texts, nor do they follow from the rest of this verse, in rhyme or in meaning. Hence I have not included them.

24

跂者不立。跨者不行。自視者不章。自見者不明。自伐者無功。自矜者不長。其在道曰。餘食贅行。物或惡之。故有道者不處。

Who tiptoes doesn't stand
who strides doesn't walk
who watches himself doesn't appear
who displays himself doesn't flourish
who flatters himself achieves nothing
who parades himself doesn't lead
on the road they say
too much food and a tiring pace
some things are simply bad
thus the Taoist shuns them

TE CH'ING says, "People raise themselves up on their tiptoes to see over the heads of others, but they cannot stand like this for long. People take longer strides to stay in front of others, but they cannot walk like this very far. Neither of these are natural."

WU CH'ENG says, "To tiptoe is to lift the heels in order to increase one's height. To stride is to extend the feet in order to increase one's pace. A person can do this for a while but not for long. Likewise, those who watch themselves don't appear for long. Those who display themselves don't flourish for long. Those who flatter themselves don't succeed for long. And those who parade themselves don't lead for long."

SU CH'E says, "Anyone can stand or walk. But if someone is not content with standing and tiptoes to extend his height or is not content with walking and strides to increase his speed, his stance and his pace are sure to suffer. It's the same with someone who watches himself, or displays himself, or flatters himself, or parades himself. It's like eating or drinking. As soon as you're full, stop. Overeating will make you ill. It's like manual work. As soon as you're done, stop. Overwork will only exhaust you."

SUNG CH'ANG-HSING says, "Selfless and free of desire is the mind of the sage. Conniving and clever is the mind of the common man. Watching himself, displaying himself, flattering himself, parading himself, he thus hastens his end, like someone who eats too much."

LI HSI-CHAI says, "Those who cultivate the Tao yet still think about themselves are like people who overeat or overwork. Food should satisfy the hunger. Work should suit the task. Those who keep to the Way do only what is natural."

LU HUI-CH'ING says, "Why should Taoists avoid things? Doesn't the Tao dwell in what others avoid? (*Taoteching*: 8). The Taoist doesn't avoid what others hate, namely humility and weakness. He only avoids what others fight over, namely flattery and ostentation. Hence he avoids some things and not others. But he never fights."

CHANG TAO-LING says, "Who follows the Way lives long. Who loses the Way dies early. This is the unbiased law of Heaven. It doesn't depend on offerings or prayers."

Line two does not appear in either Mawangtui text. The previous verse also makes do with a single-line introduction. But here the second line is needed to establish the rhyme. In line two, *k'ua:stride* can also mean "straddle." TS'AO TAO-CH'UNG says, "He who straddles two sides is unsure of the Way." Lines three through six also appear in slightly different form in verse 22, and some commentators have read 22–24 as one verse. For the wording and order of lines three through six, I have followed the Mawangtui texts, which reverse the usual order of lines three and four and which have *shih:watch* in place of the standard *shih:approve* in line three. A number of commentators think line eight is corrupt and suggest instead: "leftover food and a cyst-covered body." Although sufficiently repulsive, this is not the sort of warning we would expect of seasoned travelers of the Way. The last two lines also appear in verse 31.

25

有物混成。先天地生。蕭兮寥兮。獨立而不改。周行而不殆。可以為天下母。吾不知其名。字之曰道。吾強為之。名曰大。大曰逝。逝曰遠。遠曰反。道大。天大。地大。王亦大。國中有四大。而王居一焉。人法地。地法天。天法道。道法自然。

Imagine a nebulous thing
here before Heaven and Earth
silent and elusive
it stands alone not wavering
it travels everywhere unharmed
it could be the mother of us all
not knowing its name
I call it the Tao
forced to name it
I name it Great
great means ever-flowing
ever-flowing means far-reaching
far-reaching means returning
the Tao is great
Heaven is great
Earth is great
the king is also great
the realm contains four greats
of these the king is one
Man imitates Earth
Earth imitates Heaven
Heaven imitates the Tao
the Tao imitates itself

WU CH'ENG says, "'Nebulous' means complete and indivisible."

SU CH'E says, "The Tao is not pure or muddy, high or low, past or future, good or bad. Its body is a nebulous whole. In Man it becomes his nature.

It doesn't know it exists, and yet it endures forever. Heaven and Earth are created within it."

LI HSI-CHAI says, "It stands alone but does not stand alone. It goes everywhere but does not go anywhere. It's the mother of the world, but it is not the mother of the world."

SUNG CH'ANG-HSING says, "The Tao does not have a name of its own. We force names on it. But we cannot find anything real in them. We would do better returning to the root from which we all began."

Standing beside a stream, CONFUCIUS sighed, "To be ever-flowing like this, not stopping day or night" (*Lunyu: 9.16*).

TS'AO TAO-CH'UNG says, "Although we say it's far-reaching, it never gets far from itself. Hence we say it's returning."

HO-SHANG KUNG says, "The Tao is great because there is nothing it does not encompass. Heaven is great because there is nothing it does not cover. Earth is great because there is nothing it does not support. The king is great because there is nothing he does not control. Man should imitate Earth and be peaceful and pliant, plant it and harvest its grains, dig it and find its springs, work without exhaustion and succeed without fuss. As for Earth imitating Heaven, Heaven is still and immutable. It gives without seeking a reward. It nourishes all creatures and takes nothing for itself. As for Heaven imitating the Tao, the Tao is silent and does not speak. It directs breath and essence unseen, and thus all things come to be. As for the Tao imitating itself, the nature of the Tao is to be itself. It does not imitate anything else."

WANG PI says, "If Man does not turn his back on Earth, he brings peace to all. Hence he imitates Earth. If Earth does not turn its back on Heaven, it supports all. Hence it imitates Heaven. If Heaven does not turn its back on the Tao, it covers all. Hence it imitates the Tao. And if the Tao does not turn its back on itself, it realizes its nature. Hence it imitates itself."

Line five does not appear in either Mawangtui text. Its meaning, rhythm, and rhyme, however, all fit. Hence I have retained it.

本。躁則失君。　主。而以身輕於天下。輕則失　環官。燕處超然。如何萬乘之　子終日行。不離其輜重。雖有　重為輕根。靜為躁君。是以君

Heavy is the root of light
still is the master of busy
thus a lord might travel all day
but never far from his supplies
even in a guarded camp
his manner is calm and aloof
why would the lord of ten thousand chariots
treat himself lighter than his kingdom
too light he loses his base
too busy he loses command

HAN FEI says, "'Heavy' means controlling oneself. 'Still' means not leaving one's place. Those who are heavy control those who are light. Those who are still direct those who are busy."

WANG PI says, "Something light cannot support something heavy. Something small cannot hold down something large."

CONFUCIUS says, "A gentleman who has no weight is not held in awe, and his learning is not secure" (*Lunyu*: 1.8).

CH'ENG HSUAN-YING says, "Roots are heavy, while flowers and leaves are light. The light wither, while the heavy survive. 'Still' means tranquil, and 'busy' means excited. Excitement is subject to birth and death. Tranquility endures. Hence the still rule the busy."

TE-CH'ING says, "'Heavy' refers to the body, 'light' refers to what is external to the body: success and fame, wealth and honor. 'Still' refers to our nature, 'busy' refers to our emotions. People forget their body and chase external things. They forget their nature and follow their emotions. The sage isn't like this. Even though he travels all day, he doesn't leave what sustains him."

KUAN-TZU says, "He who moves loses his place. He who stays still remains content" (quoted by Chiao Hung).

WU CH'ENG says, "When a lord travels for pleasure, he rides in a passenger cart.

When a lord travels to war, he rides in a military cart. Both of these are light carts. And behind these come the heavier supply carts. Even though a lord might travel fifty kilometers a day in a passenger cart or thirty kilometers a day in a military cart, he does not hurry so far ahead that he loses sight of the supply carts behind him."

TS'AO TAO-CH'UNG says, "'Supplies' mean the precious commodities with which we maintain ourselves and without which we cannot exist for a second."

HO-SHANG KUNG says, "A lord who is not heavy is not respected. A plant's leaves and flowers are light, hence they are blown about by the wind. Its roots are heavy, hence it lives long. A lord who is not still loses his power. A dragon is still, hence it is able to constantly transform itself. A tiger is busy, hence it dies young."

HSUAN-TSUNG says, "Traditionally, the Son of Heaven's fief included one million neighborhoods with a tax revenue of 640,000 ounces of silver, one million cavalry horses and ten thousand war chariots. Hence he was called 'lord of ten thousand chariots.'"

SU CH'E says, "If the ruler is light, his ministers know he cannot be relied upon. If the ministers are busy, the ruler knows their minds are bent on profit."

A number of commentators have wondered if the standard *jung-kuan:glorious scenes* in line five might not be a mistake for *ying-kuan:military camp*. The Mawangtui texts have borne them out, though with *huan-kuan:guarded camp*. Line eight, which the Mawangtui texts clarify by adding *yu:than*, recalls the last four lines of verse 13. In line nine, I have gone along with the Mawangtui and Fuyi texts as well as with several early commentaries and editions in reading *pen:base* in place of *ch'en:minister.*

27

不愛其資。唯知大眯。此謂眇眇。

。故善人不善人之師。不善人善人之資。不貴其師。

是以聖人恆善救人。而無棄人。物無棄財。是謂襲明

閉者無關鍵。而不可啟。善結者無繩約。而不可解。善

善行者無徹迹。善言者無瑕讁。善數者不以籌筭。善

Good walking leaves no tracks
good talking reveals no flaws
good counting counts no beads
good closing locks no locks
and yet it can't be opened
good tying ties no knots
and yet it can't be undone
thus the sage is good at saving
and yet abandons no one
nor anything of use
this is called cloaking the light
thus the good instruct the bad
the bad learn from the good
not honoring their teachers
not cherishing their students
the wise alone are perfectly blind
this is called peering into the distance

LU TUNG-PIN says, "'Good' refers to our original nature before our parents were born. Before anything develops within us, we possess this goodness. Good means natural."

HO-SHANG KUNG says, "Someone who is good at walking finds the Way in himself, not somewhere outside. When he talks, he chooses his words. When he counts, he doesn't go beyond one. When he closes, he closes himself to desire and protects his spirit. When he ties, he ties his mind."

TE-CH'ING says, "The sage moves through the world with an empty self and accepts the way things are. Hence he leaves no tracks. He does not insist that his own ideas are right and accepts the words of others. Hence he reveals no flaws. He does not care about life and death, much less profit and loss. Hence he counts no beads. He does not set traps, and yet nothing escapes him. Hence he uses no locks. He is not kind, and yet everyone flocks to him. Hence he ties no knots."

WANG PI says, "These five tell us not to act but to govern things by relying on their nature rather than their form."

WU CH'ENG says, "The sage's salvation does not involve salvation. For if someone is saved, someone is abandoned. Hence the sage does not save anyone at all. And because he does not save anyone, he does not abandon anyone. To 'cloak' means to use an outer garment to cover an inner garment. If the work of salvation becomes apparent and people see it, it cannot be called good. Only when it is hidden is it good."

CH'ENG HSUAN-YING says, "The good always cloak their light."

HSUAN-TSUNG says, "The good are like water. Free of impurity and without effort on their part, they show people their true likeness. Thus they instruct the bad. But unless the student can forget his teacher, his vision will be obscured."

SU CH'E says, "The sage does not care about teaching, hence he does not love his students. And the world does not care about learning, hence people do not honor their teachers. The sage not only forgets the world, he makes the world forget him."

To bring out the special salvation of the sage, as explained above by Wu Ch'eng, I have used the Mawangtui connective *erh:and yet* in place of *ku:thus* in line nine. I have also used the Mawangtui version of line ten, which replaces two lines in the standard edition: "and he is good at saving things / thus he abandons nothing." For the last two characters of the last line, I have followed the word order of the Fuyi and standard editions, although I have chosen the Mawangtui *miao:peer* in place of the standard *miao:mystery* and have read the standard *yao:essential* as shorthand for *yao:distant*.

28

知其雄。守其雌。為天下奚。為天下奚。恆德不離。恆德不離。復歸於嬰
兒。知其白。守其辱。為天下谷。為天下谷。恆德乃足。恆德乃足。復歸於
朴。知其白。守其黑。為天下式。為天下式。恆德不忒。恆德不忒。復歸於
無極。朴散則為器。聖人用之則為官長。夫大制無割。

Recognize the male
but hold onto the female
and be the world's maid
being the world's maid
don't lose your ancient virtue
not losing your ancient virtue
be a newborn child again
recognize the pure
but hold onto the defiled
and be the world's valley
being the world's valley
be filled with ancient virtue
being filled with ancient virtue
be uncarved wood again
recognize the white
but hold onto the black
and be the world's guide
being the world's guide
don't stray from ancient virtue
not straying from ancient virtue
be without limits again
uncarved wood can be split to make tools
the sage makes it his chief official
a master tailor doesn't cut

TE-CH'ING says, "To recognize the Way is hard. Once you recognize it, to hold onto it is even harder. But only by holding onto it can you advance on the Way."

MENCIUS says, "The great man does not lose his child-heart" (4B.12).

WANG TAO says, "The sage recognizes 'that' but holds onto 'this.' 'Male' and 'female' refer to hard and soft. 'Pure' and 'defiled' refer to noble and humble. 'White' and 'black' refer to light and dark. Although hard, noble, and light certainly have their uses, hard does not come from hard but from soft. Noble does not come from noble but from humble. And light does not come from light but from dark. Hard, noble, and light are the secondary forms and farther from the Tao. Soft, humble, and dark are the primary forms and closer to the Tao. Hence the sage returns to the original: uncarved wood. Uncarved wood can be made into tools, but tools cannot be made into uncarved wood. The sage is like uncarved wood, not a tool. He is the chief official, not a functionary."

CH'ENG HSUAN-YING says, "What has no limits is the Tao."

CONFUCIUS says, "A great man is not a tool" (*Lunyu*: 2.12).

CHANG TAO-LING says, "To make tools is to lose sight of the Way."

SUNG CH'ANG-HSING says, "Before uncarved wood is split, it can take any shape. Once it is split, it cannot be round if it is square. It cannot be straight if it is curved. Lao-tzu tells us to avoid being split. Once we are split, we can never return to our original state."

PAO-TING says, "When I began butchering, I used my eyes. Now I use my spirit instead and follow the natural lines" (*Chuangtzu*: 3.2).

WANG P'ANG says, "Those who use the Tao to tailor leave no seams."

In lines three and four, I have followed Tunhuang copies P.2584 and S.6453 in reading *hsi:maid* for the standard *hsi:stream* as more in keeping with the images of the preceding lines. In lines eight through twenty-one, I have followed the Mawangtui texts, which fail to support the suspicions of some commentators that these lines were interpolated. Reverence for the spirit of wood is shared by many of the ethnic groups along China's borders. During Lao-tzu's day, the southern part of his home state of Ch'u was populated by the Miao, who trace their ancestry to a butterfly and the butterfly to the heart of a maple tree.

29

將欲取天下而為之。吾見其不得已。夫天下神器也。非可為者也。為者敗之。執者失之。夫物或行。或隨。或呴。或吹。或培。或墮。是以聖人去甚。去奢。去泰。

Trying to govern the world with force
I see this not succeeding
the world is a spiritual thing
it can't be forced
to force it is to harm it
to control it is to lose it
sometimes things lead
sometimes they follow
sometimes blow hot
sometimes blow cold
sometimes expand
sometimes collapse
therefore the sage avoids extremes
avoids extravagance
avoids excess

SUNG CH'ANG-HSING says, "We can't control something as insignificant as a mustard seed. How can we control something as big as the world?"

TE-CH'ING says, "Those who would govern the world should trust what is natural. The world cannot be controlled consciously. It is too big a thing. The world can only be governed by the spirit, not by human strength or knowledge."

HO-SHANG KUNG says, "Spiritual things respond to stillness. They cannot be controlled with force."

LU HUI-CH'ING says, "The world as a thing is a spiritual thing. Only the spiritual Tao can control a spiritual thing. Spiritual things don't think or act. Trying to control them with force is not the Tao."

WANG CHEN says, "'Force' refers to the mobilization and deployment of troops. But the world's spirit cannot be controlled with weapons."

LI HSI-CHAI says, "The sage considers his body transitory and the world its temporary lodging. How can he rule what is not his and lose the true and lasting Way?"

SU CH'E says, "The interchange of *yin* and *yang*, of high and low, of great and small is the way things are and cannot be avoided. Fools are selfish. They insist on having their own way and meet with disaster. The sage knows he cannot oppose things. He agrees with whatever he meets. He eliminates extremes and thereby keeps the world from harm."

WU CH'ENG says, "How does someone who gains control of the world keep the world from harm? The sage understands that things necessarily move between opposites but that there is a way to adjust this movement. Things that prosper too much must wither and die. By keeping things from prospering too much, he keeps them from withering and dying."

WANG PI says, "The sage penetrates the nature and condition of others. Hence he responds to them without force and follows them without effort. He eliminates whatever misleads or confuses them. Hence their minds become clear, and each realizes his own nature."

WANG AN-SHIH says, "Resting where you are eliminates extremes. Treasuring simplicity eliminates extravagance. Being content with less eliminates excess."

LU NUNG-SHIH says, "The sage gets rid of extremes with kindness. He gets rid of extravagance with simplicity. He gets rid of excess with humility. By means of these three, the sage governs the world."

HSUEH HUI says, "What Lao-tzu means by 'extremes,' 'extravagance,' and 'excess' is not what people mean nowadays. The Sage means whatever involves an increase in effort beyond what is easy."

For the wording of lines nine and ten, I have followed Ho-shang Kung. Between lines ten and eleven, most editions add a fourth pair of opposites: *ch'iang-lei:strengthen-weaken*. I have followed Mawangtui Text B, which has only three pairs. Given the three negations at the end of this verse, three pairs to be negated seems more appropriate.

30

以道佐人主。不以兵強於天下。其事好還。師之
所居。楚棘生之。善者果而已矣。不以取強焉。
果而勿驕。果而勿矜。果而勿伐。果而不得已矣
。是謂果而不強。物壯則老。是謂之不道。不道
早已。

Use the Tao to help your king
don't use weapons to rule the land
such things soon return
where armies camp
brambles grow
best to win then stop
don't make use of force
win but don't be proud
win but don't be vain
win but don't be cruel
win when you have no choice
this is to win without force
virility means old age
this isn't the Tao
what isn't the Tao ends early

SUNG CH'ANG-HSING says, "A kingdom's ruler is like a person's heart: when the ruler acts properly, the kingdom is peaceful. When the heart works properly, the body is healthy. What enables them to work and act properly is the Tao. Hence use nothing but the Tao to help a ruler."

LI HSI-CHAI, quoting *Mencius*: 7B.7, says, "'If you kill someone's father, someone will kill your father. If you kill someone's brother, someone will kill your brother.' This is how things return."

CH'ENG HSUAN-YING says, "The external use of soldiers and arms returns in the form of vengeful enemies. The internal use of poisonous thoughts returns in the form of evil rebirths."

WANG AN-SHIH says, "Man's retribution is clear, while Heaven's retribution is obscure. Where an army spends the night, brambles soon appear. In an army's wake, bad years follow. This is the retribution of Heaven."

Paraphrasing *Suntzu*: 2.1, WANG CHEN says, "To raise an army of a hundred thousand requires the daily expenditure of a thousand ounces of gold. And an army of a hundred thousand means a million refugees on the road. Also, nothing results in greater droughts, plagues, or famines than the scourge of warfare. A good general wins only when he has no choice, then stops. He dares not take anything by force."

MENCIUS says, "Those who say they are great tacticians or great warriors are, in fact, great criminals" (7B.2–3).

LU HUI-CH'ING says, "To win means to defeat one's enemies. To win without being arrogant about one's power, to win without being boastful about one's ability, to win without being cruel about one's achievement, this sort of victory only comes from being forced and not from the exercise of force."

SU CH'E says, "Those who possess the Tao prosper and yet seem poor, become full and yet seem empty. What is not virile does not become old and does not die. The virile die. This is the way things are. Using an army to control the world represents the height of strength. But it only hastens old age and death."

HO-SHANG KUNG says, "Once a plant reaches its height of development, it withers. Once a person reaches their peak, they grow old. Force does not prevail for long. It isn't the Tao. What is withered and old cannot follow the Tao. And what cannot follow the Tao soon dies."

WU CH'ENG says, "Those who possess the Way are like children. They age without growing old."

LAO-TZU says, "Tyrants never choose their end" (42).

I have gone along with the Mawangtui texts in omitting lines six and seven of the standard edition: "in an army's wake / bad years follow." I have also followed the Mawangtui sequence of lines eight through ten. The last three lines also appear in verse 55.

31

夫唯兵者不祥之器也。物或惡之。故有道者不處。君子居則貴左。用兵則貴右。兵者不祥之器也。故兵者非君子之器也。不得已而用之。恬惔為上。故不美也。若美之。是樂殺人。夫樂殺人。不可以得志於天下矣。是以吉事上左。凶事上右。是以偏將軍處左。上將軍處右。言以喪禮處之也。殺人眾。以悲哀泣之。戰勝。而以喪禮處之。

Weapons are not auspicious tools
some things are simply bad
thus the Taoist shuns them
in peace the ruler honors the left
in war he honors the right
weapons are not auspicious
weapons are not a ruler's tools
he wields them when he has no choice
dispassion is the best
thus he does not beautify them
he who beautifies them
enjoys killing others
he who enjoys killing others
achieves no worldly rule
thus we honor the left for joy
we honor the right for sorrow
the left is where the adjutant stands
the commander on the right
which means as at a funeral
when you kill another
honor him with your tears
when the battle is won
treat it as a wake

HO-SHANG KUNG says, "In times of decadence and disorder, we use weapons to defend the people."

SU CH'E says, "We take up weapons to rescue the distressed and not as a matter of course."

SUNG CH'ANG-HSING says, "The system of ritual devised by the ancient kings treated the right as superior and the left as inferior. Being superior, the right represented the Way of Victory. Being inferior, the left represented the Way of Humility. But victory entailed death and destruction. Hence those on the right were in charge of sad occasions, while those on the left were in charge of happy events."

JEN FA-JUNG says, "'Left' refers to the east and the power of creation, while 'right' refers to the west and the power of destruction."

HSUAN-TSUNG says, "When Tibetans, Huns, or other tribes invade the borders, the ruler has no choice but to respond. But he responds as he would to a gnat. He does not act in anger. The greatest victory involves no fighting. Hence dispassion is the best policy."

LI HSI-CHAI says, "Sun-tzu discussed in detail the use of strengths and weaknesses, of direction and indirection in warfare, but he did not understand their basis (5–6). Lao-tzu says dispassion is the best policy, for it secures victory without a display. This might seem odd, but dispassion means to rest, and rest is the root of victory. While passion means to act, and action is the basis of defeat."

KING HSIANG OF LIANG asked MENCIUS, "How can the kingdom be pacified?" Mencius answered, "The kingdom can be pacified by uniting it." King Hsiang asked, "But who can unite it?" Mencius answered, "He who does not delight in killing others can unite it" (1A.6).

LI JUNG says, "The ancients used weapons with compassion. They honored them for their virtue and disdained them as tools. Once the enemy was defeated, the general put on plain, undyed clothes, presided over a funeral ceremony, and received the mourners."

In line one, I have followed the arguments of Wang Nien-sun and Cheng Liang-shu in reading chia:fine, which precedes ping:weapons in the standard edition, as a mistake for the grammatical particle wei, which here carries no meaning. Lines two and three also appear in verse 24. For line ten, I have followed the wording of the Fuyi and Mawangtui texts, which the standard version renders: "victory is not beautiful."

32

道恆無名。朴雖小。天下莫能臣。侯王若能守之。萬物將自賓。天地相合。以渝甘露。民莫之令。而自均焉。始制有名。名亦既有。夫亦將知止。知止所以不殆。譬道之在天下也。猶川谷之與江海也。

The Tao has never had a name
simple and though small
no one can command it
if a lord upheld it
the world would be his guest
when Heaven joins with Earth
they bestow sweet dew
no one gives the order
it comes down to all
the first distinction gives us names
after we have names
we should know restraint
who knows restraint knows no trouble
to picture the Tao in the world
imagine rivers and the sea

WANG P'ANG says, "The Tao has no body. How could it have a name?"

HO-SHANG KUNG says, "The Tao can be *yin* or *yang,* it can wax or wane, it can exist or not exist. Hence it has no fixed name."

CHIAO HUNG says, "We call it 'simple' because it has not been cut or polished. We call it 'small' because it is faint and infinitesimal. Those who can see the small and hold onto it are rare indeed."

SU CH'E says, "'Simple' means the natural state. When it expands, it's everywhere. When it contracts, it isn't as big as the tip of a hair. Hence even though it is small, it is beyond anyone's command."

WANG PI says, "If someone embraces the simple and works without effort and doesn't burden their true nature with material goods or injure their spirit with desires, all things will come to them on their own, and they will discover the Tao by themselves. To discover the Tao, nothing is better than embracing simplicity."

JEN FA-JUNG says, "In terms of practice, if someone can be serene and natural, free himself from desire, and put his mind at rest, his *yin* and *yang* breaths will come together on their own and penetrate every artery and organ. Inside his mouth, the saliva of sweet dew will appear spontaneously and nourish his whole body."

LU HUI-CH'ING says, "When a ruler acts, the first thing he does is institute names."

HSUN-TZU says, "Now that the sages are gone, names and reality have become confused (22).

TE-CH'ING says, "What is simple has no name. Once we make something, we give it a name. But name gives rise to name. Where does it stop? Hence Lao-tzu tells us to stop chasing names."

TS'AO TAO-CH'UNG says, "Stop thinking and take care of your body, and you will live out your days free of trouble."

LI JUNG says, "A child who depends on its mother suffers no harm. Those who depend on the Tao encounter no trouble."

WU CH'ENG says, "The Tao has no name, but as Virtue it does. Thus from nothing we get something. But Virtue is not far from the Tao. If we stop there, we can still go from something back to nothing and return to the Tao. Thus the Tao is like the sea, and Virtue is like a river, flowing back to the Tao."

LI HSI-CHAI says, "Though Heaven and Earth are high and low, they join together and send down sweet dew. No one makes them do it. And there is no one who does not benefit. Though the Tao separates into things, and each thing has its name, the Tao never abandons anything. Thus the breath of rivers eventually reaches the sea, and the breath of the sea eventually reaches rivers."

LAO-TZU says, "The reason the sea can rule a hundred rivers / is because it has mastered being lower" (66).

Line thirteen also appears in verse 44.

33

知人者智。自知者明。勝人者有力。自勝者強。知足者富。強行者有志。不失其所者久。死而不亡者壽。

Who knows others is perceptive
who knows himself is wise
who conquers others is forceful
who conquers himself is strong
who knows contentment is wealthy
who strives hard succeeds
who doesn't lose his place endures
who dies but doesn't perish lives on

SU CH'E says, "Perception means to distinguish. Wisdom means to remove obstructions. As long as our distinguishing mind is present, we can only know others, but not ourselves."

LI HSI-CHAI says, "Perception is external knowledge. Wisdom is internal knowledge. Force is external control. Strength is internal control. Perception and force mislead us. Wisdom and strength are true. They are the door to the Tao."

HO-SHANG KUNG says, "If someone can conquer others, it is only by using force. If someone can conquer his own desires, no one in the world can compete with him. Hence we call him strong."

SUNG CH'ANG-HSING says, "The strength of those who conquer themselves is of ten kinds: the strength of faith, the strength of charity, the strength of morality, the strength of devotion, the strength of meditation, the strength of concentration, the strength of illumination, the strength of wisdom, the strength of the Way, and the strength of Virtue."

WU CH'ENG says, "Elsewhere, Lao-tzu extols simplemindedness and weakness over wisdom and strength. Why then does he extol wisdom and strength here? Wisdom and strength are for dealing with the inside. Simplemindedness and weakness are for dealing with the outside."

WANG P'ANG says, "The natural endowment of all things is complete in itself. Poverty does not reduce it. Wealth does not enlarge it. But fools abandon this treasure to chase trash. Those who know contentment pay the world no heed. This is true wealth. Mencius said, 'The ten thousand things are all within us' (7A.4). How could we not be wealthy?"

TS'AO TAO-CH'UNG says, "Though the Great Way might be far off, if we persevere without pause, we advance. We get closer and closer, until suddenly we become one with the Way. Whoever has a goal can do anything. Outside, be content with your lot. Inside, focus on the Way. And you cannot help but live long."

WANG PI says, "Those who strive with devotion reach their goal. Those who examine themselves and work within their capacity don't lose their place and are able to endure. Although we die, the Tao that gave us life doesn't perish. Our body disappears, but the Tao remains. If our body survived, would the Tao not end?"

TE-CH'ING says, "Our 'place' is like the position of the North Star. It refers to our nature."

CONFUCIUS says, "Those who govern with Virtue are like the North Star, which remains in its place, while the myriad stars revolve around it" (*Lunyu*: 2.1).

LU NUNG-SHIH says, "Before we distinguish them, life and death share the same form, the ten thousand things dwell in the same house. Our body is like the shell of a cicada or the skin of a snake: a temporary lodging. The shell perishes but not the cicada. The skin decays but not the snake. We all have something real that survives death."

KUMARAJIVA says, "Not to live in living is to endure. Not to die in dying is to live on."

Although line six seems at odds with Lao-tzu's dictum of *wu-wei:doing nothing*, the commentators are agreed that it refers to inner cultivation and not to the pursuit of worldly ambition.

34

道汎兮。其可左右。萬物恃之以生。而不
辭。成功遂事。而不名有。則恆無欲。可
名於小。萬物歸焉。而不為主。可名於大
。是以聖人終不為大。故能成其大
。

The Tao drifts
it can go left or right
everything lives by its grace
but it doesn't speak
when its work succeeds
it makes no claim
it has no desires
shall we call it small
everything turns to it
but it wields no control
shall we call it great
therefore the sage never acts great
thus he can do great things

HSUAN-TSUNG says, "To drift means to be unrestrained. The Tao is not *yin* or *yang,* weak or strong. Unrestrained, it can respond to all things and in any direction. It is not one-sided. As Chuang-tzu says, 'The Tao has no borders' (2.5)."

CHUANG-TZU also says, "Those who are skilled toil, and those who are clever worry. While those who do not possess such abilities seek nothing and yet eat their fill. They drift through life like unmoored boats" (32.1).

WANG PI says, "The Tao drifts everywhere. It can go left or right. It can go up or down. Wherever we turn to use it, it's there."

LI HSI-CHAI says, "The Great Way is a watery expanse that extends to the eight horizons. But when we use it, it's as close as our left or right hand. There is nothing that doesn't depend on it for life, and yet it never speaks of its power. There is nothing that doesn't happen without it, and yet it never mentions its achievements."

SUNG CH'ANG-HSING says, "Outside of the Tao there are no things. Outside of things there is no Tao. The Tao gives birth to things just as wind creates movement or water creates waves."

TS'AO TAO-CH'UNG says, "Though living things might be infinite in number, the Tao creates them all through the mystery of doing nothing. It doesn't mind making so many. And it creates them without thinking about its power."

WANG P'ANG says, "When the Tao becomes small, it doesn't stop being great. When it becomes great, it doesn't stop being small. But all we see are its traces. In reality, it isn't small, and it isn't great. It can't be described. It can only be known."

CH'ENG HSUAN-YING says, "The Tao produces all things, and all things turn to it. It's like the sea. All streams empty into it, and yet it doesn't control them."

Commenting on lines eight and eleven, WU CH'ENG says, "Even though there are no question indicators, these are questions and not statements, as in verse 10. If we can call something great, it isn't the Tao."

SU CH'E says, "He who is great and thinks himself great is small."

LU HUI-CH'ING says, "The Tao hides in what has no name, and the sage embodies it through what has no name. He doesn't consider himself great, and yet no one is greater. For he can go left or right. Hence he is neither small nor great. And because he is neither small nor great, he can do great things."

The Mawangtui texts omit lines three and four. Following line six, the standard edition has two additional lines: "it cares for all things / but it wields no control." But this anticipates line ten, and I have gone along with the Mawangtui texts in omitting them. For the last two lines, I have followed the standard edition. The Mawangtui texts have the more convoluted and redundant: "therefore the sage can do great things / because he does not act great / he thus can do great things."

35

執大象。天下往。往而不害。安
平泰。樂與餌。過客止。道之出
言。淡乎其無味。視之不足見
。聽之不足聞。用之不可既。

Hold up the Great Image
and the world will come
and be beyond harm
safe serene and at one
fine food and song
detain passing guests
when the Tao speaks
it's senseless and plain
we look and don't see it
we listen and don't hear it
but we use it without end

CH'ENG HSUAN-YING says, "Here 'hold' means to hold without holding, to hold what cannot be held."

HUANG YUAN-CHI says, "The Great Image is the Great Way which gives birth to Heaven and Earth and all creatures. It is called 'great' because it encompasses everything."

LI JUNG says, "The Great Image has no form. What has no form is the great and empty Way. To 'hold' means to focus or keep. Those who can keep their body in the realm of Dark Virtue and focus their mind on the gate of Hidden Serenity possess the Way. All things come to them. Clouds appear, and all creatures are refreshed. Rain pours down, and all plants are nourished. And all these blessings come from such a subtle thing."

WU CH'ENG says, "To come to no harm means to be protected. But when people turn to the sage, he uses no protection to protect them. If he protected them with protection, protection and harm would both exist. But by protecting them with no protection, they are always protected and kept from harm."

LU TUNG-PIN says, "Unharmed, our spirit is safe. Unharmed, our breath is serene. Unharmed, our nature is at one."

TE-CH'ING says, "The sage rules the world through selflessness. All things come to him because he is one with all things. And while he forgets himself in others, others forget themselves in him. Thus all things find their place, and there are none that are not at one."

CHANG TAO-LING says, "What the Tao says is the opposite of the mundane or the clever. Most people find it completely senseless. But within its senselessness, there is great sense. This is what the sage savors. The Tao prefers simplicity of form and a minimum of expression. Hence it is hard to see and hard to hear and also hard to follow. But those who can follow it and use it enjoy limitless blessings."

CHUANG-TZU says, "A great man's words are plain like water. A small man's words are sweet like wine. The plainness of a great man brings people closer, while the sweetness of a small man drives them apart. Those who come together for no reason, separate for no reason" (20.5).

SU CH'E says, "Banquets and entertainment might detain visitors, but sooner or later the food runs out, the music ends, and visitors leave. If someone entertained the world with the Great Image, no one would know how to love it, much less hate it. Although it has no taste, shape, or sound with which to please people, those who use it can never exhaust it."

HO-SHANG KUNG says, "If someone used the Tao to govern the country, the country would be rich and the people prosperous. If someone used it to cultivate himself, there would be no limit to the length of his life."

The Mawangtui texts add *ku:thus* to the beginning of line seven. I have followed the standard edition in leaving it out. Lines nine and ten are also echoed in verse 14: "we look but don't see it / and call it indistinct / we listen but don't hear it / and call it faint."

36

魚不可脫於淵。邦之利器。不可以示人。

之。必故予之。是謂微明。柔弱勝強。

故強之。將欲廢之。必故興之。將欲奪

將欲歙之。必故張之。將欲弱之。必

What you would shorten
you should therefore lengthen
what you would weaken
you should therefore strengthen
what you would topple
you should therefore raise
what you would take
you should therefore give
this is called hiding the light
the weak conquering the strong
fish can't survive out of the deep
a state's greatest tool
is not meant to be shown

TE-CH'ING says, "Once things reach their limit, they go the other way. Hence lengthening is a portent of shortening. Strengthening is the onset of weakening. Raising is the beginning of toppling. Giving is the start of taking. This is the natural order for Heaven as well as for Man. Thus to hide the light means the weak conquer the strong. Weakness is the greatest tool of the state. But a ruler must not show it to his people. Deep water is the best place for a fish. But once it is exposed to the air, a fish is completely helpless. And once a ruler shows weakness, he attracts enemies and shame."

LU HUI-CH'ING says, "To perceive shortening in lengthening, weakening in strengthening, toppling in raising, taking in giving, how could anyone do this if not through the deepest insight. This is the hidden light. Moreover, what causes things to be shortened or lengthened, weakened or strengthened, toppled or raised, taken or given is invisible and weak. While what is shortened or lengthened, weakened or strengthened, toppled or raised, taken or given is visible and strong. Thus the weak conquer the strong. People should not abandon weakness, just as fish should not abandon the depths. When fish abandon the depths, they are caught. When a person abandons weakness, he joins the league of the dead."

WU CH'ENG says, "'Hiding the light' is the same as 'cloaking the light' in verse 27.

SUNG CH'ANG-HSING says, "According to the way of the world, the weak don't conquer the strong. But Lao-tzu's point is that the weak can conquer the strong by letting the strong do what they want until they become exhausted and thus weak. Those who cultivate the Tao speak softly and act with care. They don't argue about right or wrong, better or worse. They understand the harmony of Heaven and Earth, the Way of emptiness and stillness, and become adept at using the hidden light."

CHANG TAO-LING says, "The Tao is like water. People are like fish."

CHUANG-TZU says, "The sage is the world's greatest tool but not one that is known to the world" (10.3).

HAN FEI says, "Rewards and punishments are the state's greatest tool."

Although the differences are not significant, the Mawangtui version of lines five and six abandons the rhyme. Hence I have followed the Fuyi and standard texts here. I have switched to the Mawangtui texts, however, for line ten, which the Fuyi and standard editions expand into two lines: "the soft conquer the hard / the weak conquer the strong." The copyist could have been thinking ahead to verse 78, where this couplet does, in fact, occur. Note that the appearance of *pang:state* in line twelve of the Fuyi edition and Mawangtui Text A suggests that both were copied before Liu Pang became emperor in 206 BC and made the use of his name forbidden. On the other hand, Mawangtui Text B has *kuo:country*, suggesting that it was copied after 206 BC.

道恆無為。而無不為。俟王若能守之。萬物將自化。化而欲作。吾將鎮之。以無名之朴。鎮之以無名之朴。夫將不欲。不欲以靜。天下將自正。

The Tao never does a thing
yet there is nothing it doesn't do
if a ruler could uphold it
people by themselves would change
and changing if their desires stirred
he could make them still
with simplicity that has no name
stilled by nameless simplicity
they would not desire
and not desiring be at peace
the world would fix itself

CHUANG-TZU says, "The ancients ruled the world by doing nothing. This is the Virtue of Heaven. Heaven moves without moving" (12.1).

WU CH'ENG says, "The Tao's lack of effort is ancient and eternal and not simply temporary. Although it doesn't do a thing, it does everything it should do. If rulers could uphold this Tao of effortlessness, without consciously thinking about changing others, others would change by themselves."

LAO-TZU says, "I do nothing / and the people transform themselves" (57).

TE-CH'ING says, "If nobles and kings could only uphold the Tao, all creatures would change by themselves without thinking about changing. This is the effect of upholding the Tao. When creatures first change, their desires disappear. But before long, their trust fades and feelings well up and begin to flow until desires reappear. When this occurs, those who are adept at saving others must block the source of desire with nameless simplicity."

HO-SHANG KUNG says, "'Nameless simplicity' refers to the Tao, which all creatures use to transform themselves and which nobles and kings use to pacify those who engage in cleverness and deceit."

CH'ENG HSUAN-YING says, "When people first change and begin to cultivate the Tao, they think about reaching a goal. Once this desire arises, it must be stilled with the Tao's nameless simplicity."

SU CH'E says, "The sage has no thought of embracing simplicity, nor does he show any sign of doing so. If the thought of becoming simple existed in his heart, he would miss the mark completely."

HSUAN-TSUNG says, "Once the ruler uses nameless simplicity to still the desires of the masses, he must then give it up so that they don't follow its tracks and once again enter the realm of action. Once our illness is cured, we put away the medicine. Once we are across the river, we leave the boat behind. And once we are free of desire, we must also forget the desire to be free of desire. Serene and at peace, the ruler does nothing, while the world takes care of itself."

SUNG CH'ANG-HSING says, "Other creatures follow their natures without creating chaos or disaster. They change by themselves without seeking change. People, meanwhile, race through the realm of existence and never know a quiet moment. They abandon their original innocence and don't practice the true Tao of doing nothing. They don't care about their lives, until one day they offend and retribution arrives."

The first two lines appear as one line in verse 48. The Mawangtui texts replace both lines with: "The Tao has never had a name." But this must be an interpolation from verse 32. It appears in no other edition and does not anticipate the lines that follow. Hence I have decided against it. I have also decided against the Mawangtui version where it replaces *yu:desire* with *ju:shame* in lines eight and ten and also where it replaces *t'ien-hsia:the world* with *t'ien-ti:heaven and earth* in line twelve. I have followed the Mawangtui version, however, in adding *chen-chih-yi:stilled by* to the beginning of line eight.

38

上德不德。是以有德。下德不失德。是以無德。上德無為。而無以為。上仁
為之。而無以為。上義為之。而有以為。上禮為之。而莫之應。則攘臂而扔
之。故失道而後德。失德而後仁。失仁而後義。失義而後禮。夫禮者忠信之
薄。而亂之首。前識者道之華。而愚之始。是以大丈居其厚而不居其薄。居
其實而不居其華。故去彼而取此。

Higher Virtue is not virtuous
thus it possesses virtue
Lower Virtue is not without virtue
thus it possesses no virtue
Higher Virtue lacks effort
and the thought of effort
Higher Kindness involves effort
but not the thought of effort
Higher Justice involves effort
and the thought of effort
Higher Ritual involves effort
but no response
until it threatens and compels
when the Way is lost virtue appears
when virtue is lost kindness appears
when kindness is lost justice appears
when justice is lost ritual appears
ritual marks the waning of belief
and onset of confusion
augury is the flower of the Way
and beginning of delusion
thus the great choose thick over thin
the fruit over the flower
therefore they pick this over that

HAN FEI says, "Virtue is the Tao at work."

WANG PI says, "Those who possess Higher Virtue use nothing but the Tao. They possess virtue, but they don't give it a name."

76

YEN TSUN says, "The person who embodies the Way is empty and effortless, yet he leads all creatures to the Way. The person who embodies virtue is faultless and responsive and ready to do anything. The person who embodies kindness shows love for all creatures without restriction. The person who embodies justice deals with things by matching name with reality. The person who embodies ritual is humble and reveres harmony. These five are footprints of the Tao. They are not the ultimate goal. The ultimate goal is not one, much less five."

WANG P'ANG says, "Kindness is another name for virtue. It differs, though, from virtue because it involves effort. The kindness of the sage, however, does not go beyond fulfilling his nature. He isn't interested in effort, hence he doesn't think about it."

LU HUI-CH'ING says, "Higher Kindness is kindness without effort to be kind. Kindness is simply a gift. Justice is concerned with the appropriateness of the gift. Ritual is concerned with repayment. When ritual appears, belief disappears and confusion arises."

SU CH'E says, "These are the means whereby the sage helps the people to safety. When the people don't respond, he threatens and forces them. If they still don't respond, he turns to law and punishment."

FAN YING-YUAN says, "'Augury' means to see the future. People in charge of rituals think they can see the future and devise formulas for human action but thus cause people to trade the spirit for the letter."

WU CH'ENG says, "The Tao is like a fruit. Hanging from a tree, it contains the power of life, but its womb is hidden. Once it falls, it puts forth virtue as its root, kindness as its stem, justice as its branches, ritual as its leaves, and knowledge as its flowers. All of these come from the Tao. 'That' refers to flowers. 'This' refers to fruit. Those who embody the Tao choose the fruit over the flowers."

The above categories (Higher Virtue, etc.) also appear as chapter titles in *Wentzu*. After line six, the standard and Fuyi editions add: "Lower Virtue involves effort / but not the thought of effort." But this is the same as 'Higher Kindness,' and it does not appear in the Mawangtui texts.

39

昔之得一者。天得一以清。地得一以寧。神得一以靈。谷得一以盈。侯王得一以為天下正。其致之謂。天無已清將恐裂。地無已寧將恐發。神無已靈將恐歇。谷無已盈將恐竭。侯王無已貴而高將恐蹶。故必貴以賤為本。必高以下為基。是以侯王自稱。孤寡不穀。此其賤之本歟非也。故致數輿無輿。不欲琭琭如玉。落落如石。

Of things that became one in the past
Heaven became one and was clear
Earth became one and was still
spirits became one and were active
streams became one and were full
kings became one and ruled the world
but by implication
Heaven would crack if it were always clear
Earth would crumble if it were always still
spirits would fail if they were always active
streams would dry up if they were always full
kings would fall if they were always high and noble
thus the noble is based on the humble
the high is founded on the low
thus do kings refer to themselves
as orphaned widowed and destitute
but is this the basis of humility
counting a carriage as no carriage at all
not wanting to clink like jade
they clunk like rocks

WANG PI says, "One is the beginning of numbers and the end of things. All things become complete when they become one. But once they become complete, they leave oneness behind and focus on being complete. And focusing on being complete, they lose their mother. Hence they crack, crumble, collapse, dry up, and fall. As long as they have their mother, they can preserve their form. But their mother has no form."

HO-SHANG KUNG says, "It's because Heaven becomes one that it graces the sky with constellations and light. It's because Earth becomes one that it remains still and immovable. It's because spirits become one that they change shape

78

without becoming visible. It's because streams become one that they never stop filling up. It's because kings become one that they pacify the world. But Heaven must move between *yin* and *yang*, between night and day. It can't only be clear and bright. Earth must include high and low, hard and soft, the five-fold stages of breath. It can't only be still. Spirits must have periods of quiescence. They can't only be active. Streams must also be empty and dry. They can't only be full. Kings must humble themselves and never stop seeking worthies to assist them. They can't only lord it over others. If they do, they fall from power and lose their thrones."

CHENG LIANG-SHU says, "In ancient times, kings used carriages as metaphors for the wealth and size of their kingdoms. To refer to their carriages as no carriages was an expression of self-deprecation."

SU CH'E says, "Oneness dwells in the noble, but it is not noble. Oneness dwells in the humble, but it is not humble. Oneness is not like the lustre of jade: so noble it cannot be humble, or the coarseness of rocks: so humble it cannot be noble."

Between lines five and six, the Fuyi and standard editions add the line: "all creatures became one and were alive." And between lines eleven and twelve they add: "creatures would die if they were always alive." However, neither line appears in the Yen Tsun or Mawangtui texts, and I have decided against including them. In line seven, I have also chosen the Mawangtui *wei:imply* over the standard *yi:one*. I have used the Mawangtui texts again for lines eight through twelve, where they have *wu-yi:without stop/always* in place of the usual *wu-yi:without means to*. This usage is also supported by Ho-shang Kung. For line eighteen, I have turned to the Mawangtui texts once more, along with Cheng Liang-shu's interpretation of it. The Fuyi and standard editions have: "counting their fame as no fame at all."

40

反者道之動。弱者道之用。天下之物生于有。有生于無。

The Tao moves the other way
the Tao works through weakness
the things of this world come from something
something comes from nothing

LIU CH'EN-WENG says, "Once things reach their limit, they have to go back the other way."

WEI YUAN says, "The Tao moves contrary to how most people look at things."

CH'AO CHIH-CHIEN says, "To go back the other way means to return to the root. Those who cultivate the Tao ignore the twigs and seek the root. This is the movement of the Tao—to return to where the mind is still and empty and actions soft and weak. The Tao, however, does not actually come or go. It never leaves, hence it cannot return. Only what has form returns. 'Something' refers to breath. Before things have form they have breath. Heaven and Earth and the ten thousand things are born from breath. Hence they all come from something. 'Nothing' refers to the Tao. Breath comes from the Tao. Hence it comes from nothing. This is the movement of the Tao."

WANG AN-SHIH says, "The reason the Tao works through weakness is because it is empty. We see it in Heaven blowing through the great void. We see it in Earth sinking into the deepest depths."

TE-CH'ING says, "People only know the work of working. They don't know that the work of not working is the greatest work of all. They only know that everything comes from something. They don't know that something comes from nothing. If they knew that something came from nothing, they would no longer enslave themselves to things. They would turn, instead, to the Tao and concentrate on their spirit."

HO-SHANG KUNG says, "The ten thousand things all come from Heaven and Earth. Heaven and Earth have position and form. Hence we say things come from something. The light and spirit of Heaven and Earth, the flight of insects, the movement of worms, these all come from the Tao. The Tao has no form. Hence we say things come from nothing. This means the root comes before the flower, weakness comes before strength, humility comes before conceit."

LI JUNG says, "'Something' refers to Heaven and Earth. Through the protection of Heaven and the support of Earth, all things come into being. 'Nothing' refs to the Tao. The Tao is formless and empty, and yet it gives birth to Heaven and Earth. Thus it is said, 'Emptiness is the root of Heaven and Earth. Nothingness is the source of all things.' Those who lose the Tao don't realize where things come from."

SU CH'E says, "As for the things of this world, I have heard of a mother giving birth to a child. But I have never heard of a child giving birth to its mother."

WANG PI says, "Everything in the world comes from being, and being comes from nonbeing. If you would reach perfect being, you have to go back to nonbeing."

HUANG YUAN-CHI says, "Those who cultivate the Way should act with humility and harmony. The slightest carelessness, any action at all, can destroy everything. Those who cultivate Virtue look to themselves for the truth, not to the words of others. For those who understand that what moves them is also the source of their life, the pill of immortality is not somewhere outside."

In line three, some editions add *wan:ten thousand* to *wu:things*. The Mawangtui texts reverse the order of verses 40 and 41. Also, some commentators read 40 as a continuation of 39, while others combine it with 41. *Wentzu:* 1 provides a slightly different version of the first two lines: "The Tao works through weakness / the Tao keeps moving the other way" (1).

41

上士聞道。勤而行之。中士聞道。若存若亡。下士聞道。大笑之。不笑。不足以為道。是以建言有之曰。明道若昧。進道若退。夷道若纇。上德若谷。大白若辱。廣德不足。建德若偷。質真若渝。大方無隅。大器免成。大音希聲。大象無形。道隱無名。夫唯道。善始且善成。

When a great person hears of the Way

he follows it with devotion

when an average person hears of the Way

he doesn't know if it's real or not

when a small person hears of the Way

he laughs out loud

if he didn't laugh

it wouldn't be the Way

hence these sayings arose

the brightest path seems dark

the quickest path seems slow

the smoothest path seems rough

the highest virtue low

the whitest white pitch-black

the greatest virtue wanting

the staunchest virtue timid

the truest truth uncertain

the perfect square lacks corners

the perfect tool does nothing

the perfect sound is hushed

the perfect form is shapeless

the Tao is hidden and has no name

but because it's the Tao

it knows how to start and how to finish

CONFUCIUS says, "To hear of the Tao in the morning is to die content at night-fall" (*Lunyu*: 4.8).

LI HSI-CHAI says, "When a great person hears of the Tao, even if people laugh at him, they can't keep him from practicing it. When an average person hears of the Tao, even if he doesn't disbelieve it, he can't free himself of doubts. When a small person hears of the Tao, even the ancient sages can't keep him from laughing. Everyone in the world thinks existence is real. Who wouldn't shake his head and laugh if he were told that existence wasn't real and nonexistence was?"

TE-CH'ING says, "The Tao is not what people expect. Hence the ancients created these twelve sayings, which Lao-tzu quotes to make clear that the Tao has two sides."

SU CH'E says, "These twelve sayings refer to the Tao as it appears to us. Wherever we look, we see its examples. The Tao as a whole, however, is hidden in namelessness."

LI JUNG says, "The true Tao is not fast or slow, bright or dark. It has no form, no sound, no shape, and no name. But although it has no name, it can take any name."

LU HUI-CH'ING says, "Name and reality are often at odds. The reality of the Tao remains hidden in no name."

LU HSI-SHENG says, "Tools are limited to the realm of form. The Tao is beyond the realm of form."

YEN TSUN says, "The quail runs and flies all day but never far from an overgrown field. The swan flies a thousand miles but never far from a pond. The phoenix, meanwhile, soars into the empyrean vault and thinks it too confining. Where dragons dwell, small fish swim past. Where great birds and beasts live, dogs and chickens avoid."

THE CHANKUOTSE says, "Those who know how to start don't always know how to finish" (31).

In line ten, my reading of *ju:pitch-black,* instead of the usual *ju:disgrace,* is based on the Fuyi edition. In line sixteen, I have followed Kao Heng in reading *t'ou: steal* as a loan for *ju:timid*. In the last line, I have gone along with Mawangtui Text B in reading *shih:start* instead of the usual, and puzzling, *tai:bestow*.

42

道生一。一生二。二生三。三生萬物。萬物負陰。
而抱陽。中氣以為和。天下之所惡。唯孤寡不穀。故
而王公以自名。故物或損之而益。或益之而損。
人之所教。我亦教之。強梁者不得其死。吾將以
為教父。

The Tao gives birth to one
one gives birth to two
two gives birth to three
three gives birth to ten thousand things
ten thousand things with *yin* at their backs
and *yang* in their embrace
and breath between for harmony
what the world hates
to be orphaned widowed or destitute
kings use for their titles
thus some gain by losing
others lose by gaining
thus what people teach
I teach too
tyrants never choose their deaths
this becomes my teacher

HO-SHANG KUNG says, "The Tao gives birth to the beginning. One gives birth to *yin* and *yang*. *Yin* and *yang* give birth to the breath between, the mixture of clear and turbid. These three breaths divide themselves into Heaven, Earth, and Man and together give birth to the ten thousand things. These elemental breaths are what keep the ten thousand things relaxed and balanced. The organs in our chests, the marrow in our bones, the spaces inside plants allow these breaths passage and make long life possible."

LI HSI-CHAI says, "The *yang* we embrace is one. The *yin* we turn away from is two. Where *yin* and *yang* meet and merge is three."

LU HUI-CH'ING says, "Dark and unfathomable is *yin*. Bright and perceptible is *yang*. As soon as we are born, we all turn our backs on the dark and unfathomable *yin* and turn toward the bright and perceptible *yang*. Fortunately, we keep ourselves in harmony with the breath between."

TE-CH'ING says, "'The orphaned,' 'the widowed,' and 'the destitute' are titles of self-effacement. Rulers who are not self-effacing are not looked up to by the world. Thus by losing, some people gain. Rulers who are only aware of themselves might possess the world, but the world rebels against them. Thus by gaining, some people lose. We all share this Tao, but we don't know it except through instruction. What others teach, Lao-tzu also teaches. But Lao-tzu excels others in teaching us to reduce our desires and to be humble, to practice the virtue of harmony, and to let this be our teacher."

CHIAO HUNG says, "Those who love victory make enemies. The ancients taught this, and so does Lao-tzu. But Lao-tzu goes further and calls this his 'teacher.'"

KAO HENG says, "According to the *Shuoyuan: 10.25*, 'Tyrants never choose their deaths' was an ancient saying, which Confucius attributed to the *Chinjenming*. This is what Lao-tzu refers to when he says 'what others teach.'"

WANG P'ANG says, "Whatever contains the truth can be our teacher. Tyrants kill others and are the most hated of creatures. But we can learn the principle of creation and destruction from them."

In line seven, I have followed Mawangtui Text A, which has *chung:between* in place of the usual *ch'ung:empty*. The *Yunchi Chichien* says, "When breath is pure, it becomes Heaven. When turgid, it becomes Earth. And the mixture of the breath between them becomes Man." Lines nine and ten are echoed in verse 39. In line thirteen, I have incorporated *ku:thus* from Mawangtui Text A. In line fourteen, several Tunhuang copies add *yi:justly*, while Mawangtui Text A has *yi:thoughtfully*. Both are apparently mistakes for the nearly identical *wo:I*, which appears in the Fuyi and standard editions.

43

天下之至柔。馳騁於
天下之至堅。無有入
於無間。吾是以知無
為之有益。不言之教
。無為之益。天下希
能及之矣。

The weakest thing in the world
excels the strongest thing in the world
what doesn't exist finds room where there is none
thus we know doing nothing succeeds
teaching without words
succeeding without effort
few in the world can equal this

LAO-TZU says, "Nothing in the world is weaker than water / but against the hard and the strong / nothing excels it" (78).

WANG TAO says, "Eight feet of water can float a thousand-ton ship. Six feet of leather can control a thousand-mile horse. Thus the weak excels the strong. Sunlight has no substance, yet it can fill a dark room. Thus what doesn't exist enters what has no cracks."

Concerning the first two lines, HUAI-NAN-TZU says, "The light of the sun shines across the Four Seas but cannot penetrate a closed door or a covered window. While the light of the spirit reaches everywhere and nourishes everything." Concerning the second couplet, he says, "Illumination once asked Nonexistence if it actually existed or not. Nonexistence made no response. Unable to perceive any sign of its existence, Illumination sighed and said, 'I, too, do not exist, but I cannot equal the nonexistence of Nonexistence'" (12).

LI HSI-CHAI says, "Things are not actually things. What we call 'strong' is a fiction. Once it reaches its limit, it returns to nothing. Thus the weakest thing in the world is able to overcome the strongest thing in the world. Or do you think the reality of nonexistence cannot break through the fiction of existence?"

WANG PI says, "There is nothing breath cannot enter and nothing water cannot penetrate. What does not exist cannot be exhausted. And what is perfectly weak cannot be broken. From this we can infer that doing nothing brings success."

SU CH'E says, "If we control the strong with the strong, one will break, or the other will shatter. But if we control the strong with the weak, the weak will not be exhausted, and the strong will not be damaged. Water is like this. If we use existence to enter existence, neither is able to withstand the other. But if we use nonexistence to enter existence, the former will not strain itself, while the latter will remain unaware. Spirits are like this."

HO-SHANG KUNG says, "'What doesn't exist' refers to the Tao. The Tao has no form or substance. Hence it can come and go, even where there is not any space. It can fill the spirit and help all creatures. We don't see it do anything, and yet the ten thousand things are transformed and completed. Thus we realize the benefit to mankind of doing nothing. Imitating the Tao, we don't speak. We follow it with our bodies. Imitating the Tao, we don't act. We care for ourselves, and our spirit prospers. We care for our country, and the people flourish. And we do this without effort or trouble. But few can match the Tao in caring for things by doing nothing. Lao-tzu's final 'in the world' refers to rulers."

YEN TSUN says, "Action is the beginning of chaos. Stillness is the origin of order. Speech is the door of misfortune. Silence is the gate of blessing."

TE-CH'ING says, "Words mean traces. Traces mean knowledge. Knowledge means presumption. Presumption means involvement. And involvement means failure."

One day CONFUCIUS said, "I would rather not speak." Tzu-kung asked, "If you do not speak, what will we have to record?" Confucius replied, "Does Heaven speak? The seasons travel their course, and creatures all flourish. What does Heaven say?" (*Lunyu*: 17.19).

44

名與身。孰親。身與貨。孰多。得與亡。孰病。甚愛。必大費。多藏。必厚亡。知足。不辱。知止。不殆。可以長久。

Which is more vital
fame or health
which is more precious
health or riches
which is more harmful
loss or gain
the deeper the love
the higher the cost
the bigger the treasure
the greater the loss
who knows contentment
suffers no shame
who knows restraint
encounters no trouble
and thus lives long

HUANG MAO-TS'AI says, "What the world calls fame is something external, and yet people abandon their bodies to fight for it. What the world calls riches are unpredictable, and yet people sacrifice their bodies to possess them. How can they know what is vital or precious? Even if they succeed, it's at the cost of their health."

SSU-MA KUANG says, "Which is more harmful: to gain riches and fame and lose one's health, or to gain one's health and lose riches and fame?"

LU HUI-CH'ING says, "Heroes seek fame and merchants seek riches, even to the point of giving up their lives. The one loves fame because he wants to glorify himself. But the more he loves fame, the more he loses what he would really glorify. Hence the cost is high. The other amasses wealth because he wants to enrich himself. But the more wealth he amasses, the more he harms what he would truly enrich. Hence the loss is great. Meanwhile, the man of virtue knows the most vital thing is within himself. Thus he seeks no fame and suffers no disgrace. He knows the most precious thing is within himself. Thus he seeks no riches and encounters no trouble. Hence he lives long."

LI HSI-CHAI says, "If we love something, the more we love it, the more it costs us. If we treasure something, the more we treasure it, the more it exhausts us. A little results in shame. A lot results in ruin. And regret comes too late. A wise person is not like this. He knows that he has everything he needs within himself. Hence he does not seek anything outside himself. Thus those who would shame him find nothing to shame. He knows his own limits, and his limits are the Tao. Hence he doesn't act unless according to the Tao. Thus those who would trouble him find nothing to trouble. Hence he survives and, surviving, lives long."

HO-SHANG KUNG says, "Excessive sensual desire exhausts our spirit. Excessive material desire brings us misfortune. The living keep their treasures in storerooms. The dead keep their treasures in graves. The living worry about thieves. The dead worry about grave robbers. Those who know contentment find happiness and wealth in themselves and don't exhaust their spirit. If they should govern a country, they don't trouble their people. Thus they are able to live long."

HUAI-NAN-TZU says, "Long ago Chih Po-ch'iao attacked and defeated Fan Chung-hsing. He also attacked the leaders of Han and Wei and took parts of their territories. Still he felt this wasn't enough, so he raised another army and attacked Yueh. But Han and Wei counter-attacked, and Chih's army was defeated near Chinyang, and he was killed east of Kaoliang. His skull became a drinking bowl, his kingdom was divided among the victors, and he was ridiculed by the world. This is what happens when you don't know when to stop" (18).

Some editions preface lines seven and/or eleven with *ku:thus*.

45

清靜。可以為天下正。

。大贏若絀。燥勝寒。靜勝熱。知

其用不窮。大直若屈。大巧若拙

大成若缺。其用不弊。大盈若沖

The greatest thing seems incomplete
yet it never wears out
the fullest thing seems empty
yet it never runs dry
the straightest thing seems crooked
the cleverest thing seems clumsy
the richest thing seems poor
activity overcomes cold
stillness overcomes heat
who can be perfectly still
is able to govern the world

WU CH'ENG says, "To treat the great as great, the full as full, the straight as straight, and the clever as clever is mundane. To treat what seems incomplete as great, what seems empty as full, what seems crooked as straight, what seems clumsy as clever, this is transcendent. This is the meaning of Lao-tzu's entire book: opposites complement each other."

LU NUNG-SHIH says, "The greatest thing cannot be seen in its entirety, hence it seems incomplete. The fullest thing cannot be seen in its totality, hence it seems empty. The straightest thing cannot be seen in its completeness, hence it seems crooked. The cleverest thing cannot be seen in its perfection, hence it seems clumsy."

SU CH'E says, "The world considers what is not incomplete as great, hence great includes worn out. It considers what is not empty as full, hence full includes exhausted. The sage, meanwhile, doesn't mind if the greatest thing is incomplete or the fullest thing is empty. For the greatest thing never wears out, and the fullest thing never runs dry."

HAN FEI says, "Ordinary people employ their spirit in activity. But activity means extravagance, and extravagance means wastefulness. The sage employs his spirit in stillness. Stillness means moderation, and moderation means frugality."

SUNG CH'ANG-HSING says, "We keep warm in winter by moving around. But sooner or later we stop moving and become cold again. We keep cool in summer by sitting still. But sooner or later we stop sitting still and become hot again. This is not the way of long life. This is how the great become incomplete, the full become empty, the straight become crooked, and the clever become clumsy. Those who want balance should look for it in perfect stillness. Perfect stillness is the essence of the Tao. Those who achieve such balance are free from hot and cold."

LI HSI-CHAI says, "Activity overcomes cold but cannot overcome heat. Stillness overcomes heat but cannot overcome cold. Whereas perfect stillness or lack of effort doesn't try to overcome anything, and yet nothing in the world can overcome it. Thus it is said that perfect stillness can govern the world."

CONFUCIUS says, "Those who govern with virtue are like the North Star, which remains in its place, while the myriad stars revolve around it" (*Lunyu*: 2.1).

In most editions, line seven reads: "the most eloquent thing seems dumb." I have replaced this with the version introduced by Mawangtui Text B, with which the commentary of Yen Tsun agrees. A number of commentators have had trouble making sense of lines eight and nine and have wondered if they are not corrupt. Some, for example, have suggested: "cold overcomes hot / stillness overcomes activity" as more in keeping with Lao-tzu's usage of these terms elsewhere (26, 60, and 72). I have accepted them as they stand. In line ten, I have gone along with the Fuyi text's addition of *chih:know how*. And in the last line, I have followed Mawangtui Text A in adding *k'o:able*.

46

之足。恆足矣。
足。咎莫憯於欲得。故知足
大於可欲。禍莫大於不知
下無道。戎馬生於郊。罪莫
天下有道。卻走馬以糞。天

When the Tao prevails
courier horses manure fields instead of roads
when the Tao fails
war-horses are raised on the border
no crime is worse than yielding to desire
no wrong is greater than discontent
no curse is crueler than getting what you want
the contentment of being content
is true contentment indeed

HO-SHANG KUNG says, "'When the Tao prevails' means the ruler possesses the Tao. In ordering the country, he does not use weapons, and he sends courier horses back to do farm work. In ordering himself, he redirects his *yang* essence to fertilize his body."

YEN TSUN says, "The lives of the people depend on the ruler. And the position of the ruler depends on the people. When a ruler possesses the Tao, the people prosper. When a ruler loses the Tao, the people suffer."

WANG PI says, "When the Tao prevails, contentment reigns. People don't seek external things but cultivate themselves instead. Courier horses are sent home to manure fields. When people don't control their desires, when they don't cultivate themselves but seek external things instead, cavalry horses are bred on the borders."

WU CH'ENG says, "In ancient times, every district of sixty-four neighborhoods was required to provide a horse for the army."

CHIAO HUNG says, "A 'border' refers to the land between two states. When war-horses are raised on the border, it means soldiers have not been home for a long time."

THE YENTIEHLUN says, "It is said that long ago, before the wars with the northern Hu and the southern Yueh, taxes were low, and the people were well off. Their clothes were warm, and their larders were stocked. Cattle and horses grazed in herds. Farmers used horses to pull ploughs and carts. Nobody rode them. During this period, even the swiftest horses were used to manure fields. Later, when armies arose, there were never enough horses for the cavalry, and mares were used as well. Thus, colts were born on the battlefield" (15).

LI HSI-CHAI says, "When the ruler possesses the Tao, soldiers become farmers. When the ruler does not possess the Tao, farmers become soldiers. Someone who understands the Tao turns form into emptiness. Someone who does not understand the Tao turns emptiness into form. To yield to desire means to want. Not to know contentment means to grasp. To get what you want means to possess. Want gives birth to grasping, and grasping gives birth to possessing, and there is no end to possessing. But once we know that we do not need to grasp anything outside ourselves, we know contentment. And once we know contentment, there is nothing with which we are not content."

LU HSI-SHENG says, "When the mind sees something desirable and wants it, even though it does not accord with reason, there is no worse crime. When want knows no limit, and it brings harm to others, there is no greater wrong. When every desire has to be satisfied, and the mind never stops burning, there is no crueler curse. We all have enough. When we are content with enough, we are content wherever we are."

LU TUNG-PIN says, "To know contentment means the Tao prevails. Not to know contentment means the Tao fails. What we know comes from our mind, which Lao-tzu represents as a horse. When we know contentment, our horse stays home. When we don't know contentment, it guards the border. When the Tao prevails, we put the whip away."

HSUAN-TSUNG says, "Material contentment is not contentment. Spiritual contentment is true contentment."

47

不出於戶。以知天下。不窺於
牖。以知天道。其出彌遠。其
知彌少。是以聖人不行而知。
不見而名。不為而成。

Without going out his door
he knows the whole world
without looking out his window
he knows the Way of Heaven
the farther people go
the less people know
therefore the sage knows without moving
names without seeing
succeeds without trying

CHUANG-TZU says, "Who takes Heaven as his ancestor, Virtue as his home, the Tao as his door, and who escapes change is a sage" (33.1).

HO-SHANG KUNG says, "The sage understands other persons by understanding himself. He understands other families by understanding his own family. Thus he understands the whole world. Man and Heaven are linked to each other. If the ruler is content, the breath of Heaven will be calm. If the ruler is greedy, Heaven's breath will be unstable. The sage does not have to ascend into the sky or descend into the depths to understand Heaven and Earth."

WANG PI says, "Events have a beginning. Things have a leader. Though roads diverge, they lead back together. Though thoughts multiply, they all share one thing. The Way has one constant. Reason has one principle. Holding onto the ancient Way, we are able to master the present. Though we live today, we can understand the distant past. We can understand without going outside. If we don't understand, going farther only leads us farther astray."

SU CH'E says, "The reason the sages of the past understood everything without going anywhere was simply because they kept their natures whole. People let themselves be misled by things and allow their natures to be split into ears and eyes, body and mind. Their vision becomes limited to sights, and their hearing becomes limited to sounds."

WANG P'ANG says, "If we wait to see before we become aware and wait to become aware before we know, we can see ten thousand different views and still be blind to the reason that binds them all together."

LI HSI-CHAI says, "Those who look for Heaven and Earth outside look for forms. But Heaven and Earth cannot be fathomed through form, only through reason. Once we realize that reason is right here, it doesn't matter if we close our door. For the sage, knowledge is not limited to form. Hence he doesn't have to go anywhere. Name is not limited to matter. Hence he doesn't have to look anywhere. Success is not limited to action. Hence he doesn't have to do anything."

LAO-TZU says, "The name that becomes a name / is not the Immortal Name" (1).

CH'ENG HSUAN-YING says, "'Without moving' means to know without depending on previous or external experience. 'Without seeing' means to know that everything is empty and that there is nothing to see. 'Without trying' means to focus the spirit on the tranquility that excels at making things happen."

WU CH'ENG says, "'Succeeds without trying' is the result of the previous two lines. Because the sage knows everything without going anywhere and sees everything without looking at anything, he succeeds at everything without any effort at all."

Some commentators wonder if line eight is not corrupt, if *ming:name* is not a mistake for *ming:understand,* and if the line should not instead read: "he understands without seeing." However, the only early edition that supports such an emendation is that of Han Fei. In a similar sequence, the *Chungyung* has: "flourish without any display / change without any movement / succeed without any effort" (26.6). I have retained line eight as it stands.

48

為學者日益。為道者日
損。損之又損之。以至
於無為。無為則無不為
。取天下恆無事。及其
有事。不足以取天下
。

Those who seek learning gain every day
those who seek the Way lose every day
they lose and they lose
until they find nothing to do
nothing to do means nothing not done
who rules the world isn't busy
if someone is busy
he can't rule the world

HO-SHANG KUNG says, "'Learning' refers to knowledge of administration and rhetoric, ritual and music."

CONFUCIUS asked Tzu-kung, "Do you think I learn in order to increase my knowledge?" Tzu-kung answered, "Well, don't you?" Confucius said, "No, I seek one thing that ties everything together" (*Lunyu*: 15.2).

SUNG CH'ANG-HSING says, "Those who seek the Tao don't use their ears or eyes. They look within, not without. They obey their natures, not their desires. They don't value knowledge. They consider gaining as losing and losing as gaining."

YEN TSUN says, "Get rid of knowledge. The knowledge of no knowledge is the ancestor of all knowledge and the teacher of Heaven and Earth."

WANG PI says, "Those who seek learning seek to improve their ability or to increase their mastery, while those who seek the Tao seek to return to emptiness and nothingness. When something is done, something is left out. When nothing is done, nothing is not done."

HUAI-NAN-TZU says, "The sage cultivates the inner root and does not make a display of the outer twigs. He protects his spirit and eliminates cleverness. He does nothing, which means he doesn't act until others act. And yet there is nothing that isn't done, which means he relies on the actions of others" (1).

TE-CH'ING says, "He who seeks the Tao begins by using wisdom to eliminate desires. Thus he loses. Once his desires are gone, he eliminates wisdom. Thus he loses again. And he goes on like this until the mind and the world are both forgotten, until selfish desires are completely eliminated, and he reaches the state of doing nothing. And while he does nothing, the people transform them-selves. Thus by doing nothing, the sage can do great things. Hence those who would rule the world should know the value of not being busy."

KUMARAJIVA says, "Those who lose eliminate everything coarse until they for-get about the bad, then they eliminate everything fine until they forget about the good. The bad is what they dislike. The good is what they like. First they eliminate dislikes, then they eliminate likes. Once they forget their likes and dislikes and cut themselves off from desire, their virtue becomes one with the Tao, and they reach the state of doing nothing. And while they do nothing, they let others do what they want. Hence there is nothing that isn't done."

SU CH'E says, "Everyone wants to rule the world. But when people see others doing something to possess it, they cringe. And when the people see the sage doing nothing, they rejoice. The sage doesn't seek to rule the world. The world comes to him."

TS'AO TAO-CH'UNG says, "When someone uses laws to restrict the world, might to compel it, knowledge to silence it, and majesty to impress it, there are al-ways those who don't follow. When someone rules by means of the Tao, the world follows without thinking. 'The world' refers to the ten thousand things."

WEN-TZU says, "In ancient times, those who were good rulers imitated the sea. The sea becomes great by doing nothing. Doing nothing, it governs hundreds of rivers and streams. Thus it rules by not being busy" (8).

49

聖人恆無心。以百姓之心為心。善者吾善之。不善者吾亦善之。得善矣。信者吾信之。不信者吾亦信之。得信矣。聖人之在天下歙歙焉。為天下渾心。百姓皆注其耳目。聖人皆閡之。

The sage has no mind of his own
his mind is the mind of the people
to the good he is good
to the bad he is good
until they become good
to the true he is true
to the false he is true
until they become true
in the world the sage withdraws
with others he merges his mind
people open their ears and eyes
the sage covers them up

SU CH'E says, "Emptiness has no form. It takes on the form of the ten thousand things. If emptiness had its own form it could not form anything else. Thus the sage has no mind of his own. He takes on the minds of the people and treats everyone the same."

HUI-TSUNG says, "Because it is empty, the sage's mind can receive. Because it is still, it can respond."

YEN TSUN says, "A mindless mind is the chief of all minds. The sage, therefore, has no mind of his own but embraces the minds of the people. Free of love and hate, he is not the enemy of evil or the friend of good. He is not the protector of truth or the attacker of falsehood. He supports like the earth and covers like the sky. He illuminates like the sun and transforms like the spirit."

WANG P'ANG says, "Good and bad are the result of delusions, and delusions are the result of self-centered minds. Those who open themselves up to the Great Way, though their eyes see good and bad, their minds distinguish no differences. They don't treat the bad with goodness out of pity but because they don't perceive any difference. Though the ten thousand things are different, their differences are equally real—and equally false. To see the real in the false and the false in the real is how the sage's wisdom differs from others."

CONFUCIUS says, "In his dealings with the world, the great man is neither for nor against anyone. He follows whatever is right" (*Lunyu*: 4.10).

WANG PI says, "The mind of the sage has no point of view, and his thoughts have no direction."

JEN FA-JUNG says, "Wherever the sage goes in the world, he acts humble and withdrawn and blends in with others. He treats everyone, noble or common, rich or poor, with the same kindness and equality. His mind merges with theirs. Ordinary people concentrate on what they hear and see and concern themselves with their own welfare. The sage's mind is like that of a new-born baby, pure and impartial."

HSUAN-TSUNG says, "The sage covers up the tracks of his mind by blending in with others."

CH'ENG HSUAN-YING says, "Stop the eyes and the ears, and the other senses follow."

In lines five and eight, some editions have *te:virtue* in place of *te:until*. Although the two characters were interchangeable, I have sided with the Fuyi and Yen Tsun editions in choosing "until." For lines eleven and twelve, most commentators read: "the people focus their ears and eyes on him / and the sage treats them like babies." But in verses 10, 20, 28, and 55, Lao-tzu likens the sage, not the people, to a child, and I suspect the text is corrupt here. Unfortunately, both Mawangtui texts are indecipherable, while the Fuyi variation of *k'o:cough*, the Tunhuang variation of *hai:suffer*, and Yen Tsun's *hai:startle* are clearly loans. But loans for what? Most commentators argue for *hai:infant*. I've gone along with Kao Heng, who suggests *ai:obstruct*.

50

故
。
以
其
無
死
地
。

無
所
投
其
角
。
虎
無
所
措
其
爪
。
兵
無
所
容
其
刃
。
夫
何

蓋
聞
善
攝
生
者
。
陵
行
不
遇
兕
虎
。
入
軍
不
被
甲
兵
。
兕

生
生
。
動
皆
之
死
地
之
十
有
三
。
夫
何
故
。
以
其
生
生
。

出
生
。
入
死
。
生
之
徒
十
有
三
。
死
之
徒
十
有
三
。
而
民

Appearing means life
disappearing means death
thirteen are the followers of life
thirteen are the followers of death
but people living to live
join the land of death's thirteen
and why
because they live to live
it's said that those who guard life well
aren't injured by soldiers in battle
or harmed by rhinos or tigers in the wild
for rhinos have nowhere to sink their horns
tigers have nowhere to sink their claws
and soldiers have nowhere to sink their blades
and why
because for them there is no land of death

CH'ENG CHU says, "Of the ten thousand changes we all experience, none are more important than life and death. People who cultivate the Tao are concerned with nothing except transcending these boundaries."

In lines three, four, and six, the phrase *shih-yu-san* has long puzzled commentators. HAN FEI says it means "three and ten" or "thirteen" and refers to the four limbs and nine orifices of the body, which can be guarded to preserve life or indulged to end it.

TU ER-WEI also reads "thirteen" but sees its numerical significance in the moon, which becomes full thirteen days after it first appears and which disappears after another thirteen days.

WANG PI says it means "three in ten" and refers to three attitudes toward life among ten people. WANG AN-SHIH summarizes these as: "Some seek life because they hate death, some seek death because they hate life, and some live as if they were dead." The remainder belongs to the sage, who neither hates death nor loves life, but who lives long.

The Mawangtui texts, which I have followed, word lines five and six in such a way as to make Wang Pi's interpretation unlikely, if not impossible. As for choosing between Han Fei and Tu Er-wei, I think Tu's interpretation comes closer to what Lao-tzu had in mind.

WANG PI says, "Eels consider the depths too shallow, and eagles consider the mountains too low. Living beyond the reach of arrows and nets, they dwell in the land of no death. But by means of bait, they are lured into the land of no life."

SU CH'E says, "We know how to act but not how to rest. We know how to talk but not how to keep still. We know how to remember but not how to forget. Everything we do leads to the land of death. The sage dwells where there is neither life nor death."

TE-CH'ING says, "Those who guard their life don't cultivate life but what controls life. What has life is form. What controls life is nature. When we cultivate our nature, we return to what is real and forget bodily form. Once we forget form, our self becomes empty. Once our self is empty, nothing can harm us. Once there is no self, there is no life. How could there be death?"

CHIAO HUNG says, "The sage has no life. Not because he slights it, but because he doesn't possess it. If someone has no life, how can he be killed? Those who understand this can transcend change and make of life and death a game."

I have followed the Mawangtui wording of lines five, six, and also eight, to which some editions add the phrase *chih-hou:to excess,* while others add the last two lines of verse 75 as well. Although soldiers are still plentiful in China, tigers are rare, and rhinos limited to the imagination of a zoologist I met in Sian at the Chinese Academy of Science, who reports seeing them in the nearby Chinling Range.

51

道生之。德畜之。物形之。器成之。是以萬物尊道。而貴德。道之尊。德之貴。夫莫之爵。而恆自然。道生之畜之。長之育之。亭之毒之。養之覆之。生而不有。為而不恃。長而不宰。是謂玄德。

The Way begets them
Virtue keeps them
matter shapes them
usage completes them
thus do all things honor the Way
and glorify Virtue
the honor of the Way
the glory of Virtue
are not conferred
but always so
the Way begets and keeps them
cultivates and trains them
steadies and adjusts them
nurtures and protects them
but begets without possessing
acts without presuming
and cultivates without controlling
this is called Dark Virtue

WU CH'ENG says, "What is begotten is sprouted in spring; what is kept is collected in fall; what is shaped is raised in summer from sprouts grown in spring; what is completed is stored in winter from the harvest of fall. Begetting, raising, harvesting, and storing all depend on the Way and Virtue. Hence the ten thousand things honor the Tao as their father and glorify Virtue as their mother. The Way and Virtue are two, but also one. In spring, from one root many are begotten: the Way becomes Virtue. In fall, the many are brought back together: Virtue becomes the Way. The Way and Virtue are mentioned at the beginning of this verse, but only the Way is mentioned later. This is because Virtue is also the Way."

LI HSI-CHAI says, "What the Way and Virtue bestow, they bestow without thought. No one orders them. It is simply their nature. It is their nature to beget and their nature to keep. It is their nature to cultivate and train, to steady and adjust, to nurture and protect. And because it's their nature, they never tire of begetting or expect a reward for what they give. This is what is meant by 'Dark Virtue.'"

LU HSI-SHENG says, "To beget is to endow with essence. To keep is to instill with breath. To cultivate is to adapt to form. To train is to bring forth ability. To steady is to weigh the end. To adjust is to measure the use. To nurture is to preserve the balance. To protect is to keep from harm. This is the Great Way. It begets but does not try to possess what it begets. It acts but does not presume on what it does. It cultivates but does not try to control what it cultivates. This is Dark Virtue. In verse 10, Man is likened to the Way and Virtue. Here, the Way and Virtue are likened to Man. The expressions are the same, and so is the meaning."

HO-SHANG KUNG says, "The Way does not beget the myriad creatures to possess them for its own advantage. The actions of the Way do not depend on a reward. And the Way does not cultivate or nurture the myriad creatures to butcher them for profit. The kindness performed by the Way is dark and invisible." Where Ho-shang Kung reads "butcher," Lu Hsi-sheng reads "control." I have followed Lu.

WANG PI says, "The Way is what things follow. Virtue is what they attain. 'Dark Virtue' means virtue is present but no one knows who controls it. It comes from what is hidden."

In line four, I have followed the Mawangtui texts in reading *ch'i:usage* for *shih:condition.* I have also gone along with the Mawangtui texts in omitting *mo-pu:none does not* from line five and in using their version of line twelve, in which *ting:steady* and *tu:adjust* appear in place of *ch'eng:mature* and *shu:ripen.*

52

天下有始。以為天下母。既得其母。以知其子。既知其子。
復守其母。沒身不殆。塞其兌。閉其門。終身不勤。開其
兌。濟其事。終身不救。見小曰明。守柔曰強。用其光。復
歸其明。無遺身殃。是謂襲常。

The world has a maiden
she becomes the world's mother
who knows the mother
understands the child
who understands the child
keeps the mother safe
and lives without trouble
who blocks the opening
who closes the gate
lives without toil
who unblocks the opening
who meddles in affairs
lives without hope
who sees the small has vision
who protects the weak has strength
who uses his light
who trusts his vision
lives beyond death
this is the Hidden Immortal

LAO-TZU says, "The maiden of Heaven and Earth has no name / the mother of all things has a name" (1).

KUAN-TZU says, "The ancients say, 'No one understands a child better than its father. No one understands a minister better than his ruler'" (7).

LI HSI-CHAI says, "The Way is the mother of all things. Things are the children of the Way. In ancient times, those who possessed the Way were able to keep mother and children from parting and the Way and things together. Since things come from the Way, they are no different from the Way, just as children are no different from their mother. And yet people abandon things when they search for the Way. Is this any different from abandoning the children while searching for the mother? If people knew that things are the Way, and children are the mother, they would find the source in everything they meet."

CONFUCIUS says, "Things have their roots and branches. Those who know what comes first and last approach the Tao (*Tahsueh*: intro.).

TUNG SSU-CHING says, "People are born when they receive breath. Breath is their mother. And spirit dwells in their breath. When children care for their mother, their breaths become one and their spirits become still."

WU CH'ENG says, "'Opening' refers to the mouth. 'Gate' refers to the nose. By controlling our breath to the point where there is no breath, where breath is concentrated within, we are never exhausted."

WANG P'ANG says, "When the opening opens, things enter. And the spirit is exhausted trying to deal with the problems that develop. Once we are swept away by this flood, who can save us?"

HSUAN-TSUNG says, "If someone can see an event while it is still small and can change his behavior, we say he has vision."

WANG PI says, "Seeing the great is not vision. Seeing the small is vision. Protecting the strong is not strength. Protecting the weak is strength."

WANG AN-SHIH says, "Light is the function of vision. Vision is the embodiment of light. If we can use the light to find our way back to the source, we can live our lives free of misfortune and become one with the Immortal Way."

While translating this verse, I have often recalled Confucius' words: "When I was young, historians still left blanks" (*Lunyu*: 15.25). Not being a historian, I have proceeded despite uncertainty. In the last line, I have based my reading of *ch'ang:immortal*, in place of the usual *constant*, on the fact that *ch'ang* is also the name of the Spirit of the West, namely the new and reborn moon.

53

使我介有知。行於大道。唯迤是畏。大道甚
夷。而民好徑。朝甚除。田甚蕪。倉甚虛。
服文采。帶利劍。厭飲食。貨財有餘。是謂
盜夸。盜夸非道哉。

Were I sufficiently wise
I would follow the Great Way
and only fear going astray
the Great Way is smooth
but people love byways
their palaces are spotless
their fields are overgrown
their granaries are empty
they wear fine clothes
and carry sharp swords
they tire of food and drink
and possess more than they need
this is called robbery
and robbery is not the Way

KU HSI-CH'OU says, "The Tao is not hard to know, but it is hard to follow."

HO-SHANG KUNG says, "Lao-tzu was concerned that rulers of his day did not follow the Great Way. Hence he hypothesized that if he knew enough to conduct the affairs of a country, he would follow the Great Way and devote himself to implementing the policy of doing nothing."

LU HSI-SHENG says, "The Great Way is like a grand thoroughfare: smooth and easy to travel, perfectly straight and free of detours, and there is nowhere it doesn't lead. But people are in a hurry. They take shortcuts and get into trouble and become lost and don't reach their destination. The sage only worries about leading people down such a path."

LI HSI-CHAI says, "A spotless palace refers to the height of superficiality. An overgrown field refers to an uncultivated mind. An empty granary refers to a lack of virtue."

HAN FEI says, "When the court is in good repair, lawsuits abound. When lawsuits abound, fields become overgrown. When fields become overgrown, granaries become empty. When granaries become empty, the country becomes poor. When the country becomes poor, customs become decadent, and there is no trick the people don't try."

SUNG CH'ANG-HSING says, "When the court ignores the affairs of state to beautify its halls and interrupts farmwork to build towers and pavilions, the people's energy ends up at court, and fields turn to weeds. Once fields turn to weeds, state taxes are not paid and granaries become empty. And once granaries are empty, the country becomes poor, and the people become rebellious. When the court dazzles the people with fine clothes, and threatens the people with sharp swords, and takes from the people more than it needs, this is no different than robbing them."

LI JUNG says, "A robber is someone who never has enough and who takes more than he needs."

WANG PI says, "To gain possession of something by means other than the Way is wrong. And wrong means robbery."

WANG NIEN-SUN sees a problem with the standard version of line three, which reads: "and only fear acting." Wang suggests *shih:act* should read *yi:go astray*. The Mawangtui texts have *t'a:he*, which is clearly a mistake but which makes *yi* just as likely as *shih*. All three characters are nearly identical. Further support for Wang's suggested emendation comes from the connection it provides between line three and lines four and five, all of which share a common rhyme.

In the last two lines, *tao:rob* is followed by *k'ua:grand* in the Fuyi edition and blank text in the Mawangtui editions. I have read *k'ua* as a mistake for a nearly identical character: *hsi,* which functions like a comma and which provides a sharper delineation of the Chinese pun in which *robbery* and *Way* are homophones.

54

善建者不拔。善抱者不脫。子孫以祭祀不絕。修之身其德乃真。修之家其德乃餘。修之鄉其德乃長。修之邦其德乃豐。修之天下其德乃博。故以身觀身。以家觀家。以鄉觀鄉。以邦觀邦。以天下觀天下。吾何以知天下之然。以此。

What is planted right is not uprooted
what is held right is not ripped away
future generations worship it forever
cultivated in the self virtue becomes real
cultivated in the family virtue multiplies
cultivated in the village virtue increases
cultivated in the state virtue prospers
cultivated in the world virtue abounds
thus view the self through the self
view the family through the family
view the village through the village
view the state through the state
view the world through the world
how do we know what the world is like
through this

WU CH'ENG says, "Those who plant it right, plant without planting. Thus it is never uprooted. Those who hold it right, hold without holding. Thus it is never ripped away."

WANG AN-SHIH says, "What we plant right is virtue. What we hold right is oneness. When virtue flourishes, distant generations give praise."

TS'AO TAO-CH'UNG says, "First improve yourself, then reach out to others, and to later generations bequeath the noble, pure, and kindly Tao. Thus blessings reach your descendants, virtue grows, beauty lasts, and worship never ends."

SUNG CH'ANG-HSING says, "In ancient times, ancestral worship consisted in choosing an auspicious day before the full moon, in fasting, in selecting sacrificial animals, in purifying the ritual vessels, in preparing a feast on the appointed day, in venerating ancestors as if they were present, and in thanking them for their virtuous example. Those who cultivate the Way likewise enable later generations to enjoy the fruits of their cultivation."

HO-SHANG KUNG says, "We cultivate the Tao in ourselves by cherishing our breath and by nourishing our spirit and thus by prolonging our life. We cultivate the Tao in the family by being loving as a parent, filial as a child, kind as an elder, obedient as the younger, dependable as a husband, and chaste as a wife. We cultivate the Tao in the village by honoring the aged and caring for the young, by teaching the benighted and instructing the perverse. We cultivate the Tao in the state by being honest as an official and loyal as an aide. We cultivate the Tao in the world by letting things change without giving orders. Lao-tzu asks how we know that those who cultivate the Tao prosper and those who ignore the Tao perish. We know by comparing those who don't cultivate the Tao with those who do."

YEN TSUN says, "Let your body be the yardstick of other bodies. Let your family be the level of other families. Let your village be the square of other villages. Let your state be the plumb line of other states. As for the world, the ruler is its heart, and the world is his body."

CHUANG-TZU says, "The reality of the Tao lies in concern for the self. Concern for the state is irrelevant, and concern for the world is cowshit. From this standpoint, the emperor's work is the sage's hobby and is not what develops the self or nourishes life" (28.3).

As in verse 36, Mawangtui Text A has *pang:state*, while Mawangtui Text B has the synonym *kuo:country*, suggesting Text A was copied before 206 BC and Text B was copied later. In line nine, both Mawangtui texts omit *ku:thus*, while the Fuyi and standard editions include it.

55

含德之厚者。比於赤子。蜂蠆不螫。猛獸不攫。鷙鳥不搏。骨
弱筋柔。而握固。未知牝牡之合。而朘作。精之至。終日號。
而不嗄。和之至。知和曰常。知常曰明。益生曰祥。心使氣
曰強。物壯則老。謂之不道。不道早已。

He who contains virtue in abundance
resembles a newborn child
wasps don't sting him
beasts don't claw him
birds of prey don't carry him off
his bones are weak his tendons are soft
and yet his grip is firm
he hasn't known the union of sexes
and yet his penis is stiff
so full of essence is he
he cries all day
yet never gets hoarse
so full of breath is he
who knows how to breathe endures
who knows how to endure is wise
who lengthens his life tempts luck
who breathes with his will is strong
but virility means old age
this isn't the Way
what isn't the Way ends early

WANG P'ANG says, "The nature of virtue is lasting abundance. But its abundance fades with the onset of thoughts and desires."

SU CH'E says, "Once we have a mind, we have a body. And once we have a body, we have enemies. If we did not have a mind, we would not have enemies and could not be harmed. The reason a newborn child is not harmed is because it has no mind."

HO-SHANG KUNG says, "A newborn child doesn't harm anyone, and no one harms it. In an age of perfect peace, mankind knows neither noble nor base. Even wild beasts do people no harm."

TE-CH'ING says, "Those who cultivate the Tao should first focus their minds. When the mind doesn't stray, it becomes calm. When the mind becomes calm, breath becomes balanced. When breath becomes balanced, essence becomes stable, spirit becomes serene, and our true nature is restored. Once we know how to breathe, we know how to endure. And once we know how to endure, we know our true nature. If we don't know our true nature but only know how to nourish our body and lengthen our lives, we end up harming our body and destroying our lives. A restless mind disturbs the breath. When the breath is disturbed, the essence weakens. And when the essence weakens, the body withers."

HSUN-TZU says, "Everything must breathe to live. When we know how to breathe, we know how to nurture life and how to endure" (17).

SUNG CH'ANG-HSING says, "The basis of life rests on this breath. If someone can nourish the pure and balanced breath within himself for fifteen minutes, he will discover the principle of Heaven and Earth's immortality. If he can do this for half an hour, he will enter the gate of eternity. But if he tries to extend his life or force his breath, he will create the womb of his destruction."

WANG AN-SHIH says, "Life cannot be extended. But people keep trying and thus incur misfortune."

MOU-TZU says, "Those who attain the Way don't become active and don't become strong. They don't become strong and don't become old. They don't become old and don't become ill. They don't become ill and don't decay. Thus Lao-tzu calls the body a disaster" (32).

The Mawangtui texts compress lines three through five into two lines. In lines thirteen and fourteen, I have followed *Huainantzu: 2* and *Huangti Neiching: 69–70* in reading *ho:gentle* as short for *ho-ch'i:gentle breath*. Line fifteen also appears in verse 16, and the last three lines also occur at the end of verse 30.

56

知者不言。言者不知。塞其兌。閉其門。挫其銳。解
其紛。和其光。同其塵。是謂玄同。不可得而親。亦
不可得而疏。不可得而利。亦不可得而害。不可得
而貴。亦不可得而賤。故為天下貴。

Those who know don't talk

those who talk don't know

seal the opening

close the gate

dull the edge

untie the tangle

soften the light

join the dust

this is called the Dark Union

it can't be embraced

it can't be abandoned

it can't be helped

it can't be harmed

it can't be exalted

it can't be debased

thus does the world exalt it

HO-SHANG KUNG says, "Those who know, value deeds not words. A team of horses can't overtake the tongue. More talk means more problems."

TS'AO TAO-CH'UNG says, "Those who grasp the truth forget about words. Those who don't practice what they talk about are no different from those who don't know."

SU CH'E says, "The Tao isn't talk, but it doesn't exclude talk. Those who know don't necessarily talk, and those who talk don't necessarily know."

HUANG YUAN-CHI says, "We seal the opening and close the gate to nourish the breath. We dull the edge and untie the tangle to still the spirit. We soften the light and join the dust to adapt to the times and flow with the world."

LI HSI-CHAI says, "By sealing the opening, we guard the exit. By closing the gate, we bar the entrance. By dulling the edge, we adjust the inside. By untying the tangle, we straighten the outside. By softening the light, we focus on ourselves. By joining the dust, we adapt to others. What is devoid of exit and entrance, inside and outside, self and other, we call the Dark Union."

WANG TAO says, "The Dark Union unites all things but leaves no visible trace."

WANG PI says, "If something can be embraced, it can be abandoned. If something can be helped, it can be harmed. If something can be exalted, it can be debased."

TE-CH'ING says, "The sage transcends the mundane and the superficial, hence he cannot be embraced. His utter honesty enables others to see, hence he cannot be abandoned. He is content and free of desires, hence he cannot be helped. He dwells beyond life and death, hence he cannot be harmed. He views high position as so much dust, hence he cannot be exalted. Beneath his rags he harbors jade, hence he cannot be debased. The sage walks in the world, yet his mind transcends the material realm. Hence he is exalted by the world."

WEI YUAN says, "Those who seal the opening and close the gate don't love or hate, hence they don't embrace or abandon anything. Those who dull the edge and untie the tangle don't seek help, and thus they suffer no harm. Those who soften the light and join the dust don't exalt themselves, and thus they aren't debased by others. Forgetting self and other, they experience Dark Union with the Tao. Those who haven't yet experienced this Dark Union unite with 'this' and separate from 'that.' To unite means to embrace, to help, to exalt. To separate means to abandon, to harm, to debase. Those who experience Dark Union unite with nothing. From what, then, could they separate?"

Lines three and four also occur in verse 52, and lines five through eight appear in verse 4 as well. The Mawangtui texts begin line ten with *ku:thus*.

57

以正治邦。以奇用兵。以無事取天下。吾何以知其然哉。夫天下多

忌諱。而民彌貧。民多利器。而邦家滋昏。民多智巧。而奇物滋

起。法物滋彰。而盜賊多有。是以聖人之言曰。我無為。而民自

化。我好靜。而民自正。我無事。而民自富。我無欲。而民自朴。

Use direction to govern a country
use indirection to fight a war
use inaction to rule the world
how do we know this works
the greater the prohibitions
the poorer the people
the sharper the weapons
the darker the realm
the smarter the scheme
the stranger the outcome
the finer the treasure
the thicker the thieves
thus the sage declares
I change nothing
and the people transform themselves
I stay still
and the people adjust themselves
I do nothing
and the people enrich themselves
I want nothing
and the people simplify themselves

SUN-TZU says, "In waging war, one attacks with direction, one wins with indirection" (5.5).

WANG AN-SHIH says, "Direction can be used in governing, but nowhere else. Indirection can be used in warfare, but that is all. Only those who do nothing are fit to rule the world."

SU CH'E says, "The ancient sages were kind to strangers and gentle to friends. They didn't think about warfare. Only when they had no choice did they fight.

And when they did, they used indirection. But indirection can't be used to rule the world. The world is a mercurial thing. To conquer it is to lose it. Those who embody the Tao do nothing. They don't rule the world, and yet the world comes to them."

LU HUI-CH'ING says, "How do we know that we can rule the world by means of inaction? Because we know that we cannot rule the world by means of action."

TE-CH'ING says, "Prohibitions, weapons, schemes, treasures, all of these involve action and cannot be used to rule the world."

WANG PI says, "Prohibitions are intended to put an end to poverty, and yet the people become poorer. Weapons are intended to strengthen the country, and yet the country becomes weaker and more confused. This is due to cultivating the branches instead of the roots."

WANG P'ANG says, "Prohibitions interfere with the people's livelihood. Thus poverty increases. Sharp weapons mean sharp minds. And sharp minds mean darkness and chaos. Once minds become refined, customs become depraved, and the unusual becomes commonplace."

HO-SHANG KUNG says, "In cultivating the Tao, the sage accepts the will of Heaven. He doesn't change things, and the people transform themselves. He prefers not to talk or teach, and the people correct themselves. He doesn't force others to work, and the people become rich at their occupations. He doesn't use ornaments or luxuries, and the people emulate his simple ways."

CONFUCIUS says, "The virtue of the ruler is like wind. The virtue of the people is like grass. When the wind blows, the grass bends" (*Lunyu*: 12.19).

At the end of line four, the Fuyi, Suotan, and standard editions answer with: *yi-tz'u:because of this*. I have followed the Mawangtui texts, which omit this phrase. In most editions, line eleven has *fa-ling:laws and orders*. I have gone along with Mawangtui Text B and Ho-shang Kung, both of which have *fa-wu:fine things*.

58

其政悶悶。其民淳淳。其政察察。其民缺缺。禍兮
福之所倚。福兮禍之所伏。孰知其極。其無正也。
正復為奇。善復為妖。民之迷也。其日固久矣。是以
聖人方而不割。廉而不劌。直而不肆。光而不曜。

Where government stands aloof
the people open up
where government steps in
the people slip away
happiness rests in misery
misery hides in happiness
who knows where they end
there is no direction
direction turns into indirection
good turns into evil
the people have been lost
for a long long time
thus the sage is an edge that doesn't cut
a point that doesn't pierce
a line that doesn't extend
a light that doesn't blind

HSUAN-TSUNG says, "To stand aloof is to be relaxed and unconcerned. To open up is to be simple and honest. The ruler who governs without effort lets things take care of themselves."

WANG PI says, "Those who are good at governing use neither laws nor measures. Thus the people find nothing to attack."

LI HSI-CHAI says, "When the government makes no demands, the people respond with openness instead of cleverness. When the government makes demands, the people use every means to escape. The government that stands aloof leaves power with the people. The government that steps in takes their power away. As one gains, the other loses. As one meets with happiness, the other encounters misery."

WANG P'ANG says, "Everything shares the same breath. But the movement of this breath comes and goes. It ends only to begin again. Hence happiness and misery alternate like the seasons. But only the sage realizes this. Hence in everything he does, he aims for the middle and avoids the extremes, unlike the government that insists on direction and goodness and forbids indirection and evil, the government that wants the whole world to be happy and yet remains unaware that happiness alternates with misery."

LU NUNG-SHIH says, "Only those who are free of direction can transcend the appearance of good and evil and eliminate happiness and misery. For they alone know where these end. Meanwhile, those who cannot reach the state where there is no direction, who remain in the realm of good and evil, suffer happiness and misery as if they were on a wheel that carries them farther astray."

TE-CH'ING says, "The world withers, and the Tao fades. People are not the way they once were. They don't know direction from indirection or good from evil. Even the sage cannot instruct them. Hence to transform them, he enters their world of confusion. He joins their dust and softens his light. And he leaves no trace."

WU CH'ENG says, "The sage's inaction is inaction that is not inaction. Edges always cut. But the edge that is not an edge doesn't cut. Points always pierce. But the point that is not a point doesn't pierce. Lines always extend. But the line that is not a line doesn't extend. Lights always blind. But the light that is not a light doesn't blind. All of these are examples of inaction."

Most editions make it possible to read line eight as a question or a statement. I have followed Mawangtui Text B, which words it as a statement. In line thirteen, Text B omits *sheng-jen:the sage*. Line fourteen also appears in the *Lichi*: "The gentleman compares his virtue to that of jade: pointed but not piercing" (48). And line fifteen recalls verse 45: "the straightest thing seems crooked." Wu Ch'eng combines this with the previous verse.

59

治人事天。莫若嗇。夫唯嗇是
以早服。早服是謂重積德。重
積德則無不剋。無不剋則莫知
其極。莫知其極可以有國。有
國之母可以長久。是謂深根
固柢。長生久視之道。

In governing people and caring for Heaven
nothing surpasses economy
economy means planning ahead
planning ahead means accumulating virtue
accumulating virtue means overcoming all
overcoming all means knowing no limit
knowing no limit means guarding the realm
guarding the realm's mother means living long
this means deep roots and a solid trunk
the Way of long and lasting life

LI HSI-CHAI says, "Outside, we govern others. Inside, we care for Heaven. In both, nothing surpasses economy. Those who are economical are economical in everything. They're watchful within and on guard without. Only if we are still, does virtue have a place to collect."

MENCIUS says, "The way we care for Heaven is by guarding our minds and nourishing our natures" (7A.1).

WANG TAO says, "Caring for Heaven means preserving what one receives from Heaven. It means cultivating oneself."

Linking this with the previous verse, SU CH'E says, "Economy is the reason the sage's edges don't cut, his points don't pierce, his lines don't extend, and his light doesn't blind. Economy means possessing without using."

WANG PI says, "Economy means farming. Farmers cultivate their fields by weeding out different species and concentrating on one thing. They don't worry about pulling out the withered and diseased. They pull out the causes of withering and disease. Above, they accept the will of Heaven. Below, they nourish the people."

HAN FEI says, "Most people use their minds recklessly. Recklessness means waste, and waste means exhaustion. The sage uses his mind calmly. Calmness means carefulness, and carefulness means economy. Economy is an art born of an understanding of the Tao. Those who know how to govern others calm their thoughts. Those who know how to care for Heaven clear their openings.

When thoughts are calm, old virtue remains within. When openings are clear, new breath enters from without."

HO-SHANG KUNG says, "Someone whose virtue knows no limits can guard the gods of the realm and bring happiness to the people."

THE LICHI says, "He who guards the realm is ever careful" (27).

LI JUNG says, "When the ruler maintains the Tao, the country is at peace. When he fails to maintain the Tao, the country is in chaos. The country is the offspring. The Tao is the mother."

WU CH'ENG says, "The realm is a metaphor for the body. Breath is the body's mother. Breath that has no limit can preserve the body. Someone who fills themselves with breath can conquer the world and remain unharmed. Breath rises from below as if from the roots of a tree. By nourishing the roots, the roots grow deep. Breath flourishes above as the trunk of a tree does. By nourishing the trunk, the trunk grows firm. Thus the tree doesn't wither."

LU NUNG-SHIH says, "The roots are in the dark, and the trunk is in the light. The roots refer to life, and the trunk refers to nature. What nothing can fathom is deep. Only life can match this. What nothing can topple is firm. Only nature can match this."

In line two, *shih:pattern* appears in some editions instead of *se:economy*. Also, in lines three and four, *fu:return* appears in some texts in place of *fu:subdue/plan*. In both cases, I have followed the Fuyi and Suotan editions as well as Mawang-tui Text B in choosing the latter. The last line appears as a saying in other ancient texts, including *Hsuntzu: 4* and *Lushih Chunchiu:* 1.3, in which commentators interpret *shih:vision* as a cliche for "life."

60

治大國。若亨小鮮。以道莅天下
。其鬼不神。非其鬼不神。其神
不傷人。非其神不傷人。聖人亦
不傷人。夫兩不相傷。故德交歸
焉。

Ruling a great state
is like cooking a small fish
when you govern the world with the Tao
spirits display no powers
not that they display no powers
their powers do people no harm
not that their powers do people no harm
the sage does people no harm
and neither harms the other
for both rely on Virtue

In a poem bemoaning the absence of virtuous leaders, THE SHIHCHING says, "Who can cook fish / I'll wash out the pot" (Kuei.4).

LI HSI-CHAI says, "For the sage, ruling a state is a minor affair, like cooking a small fish."

HO-SHANG KUNG says, "If you cook a small fish, don't remove its entrails, don't scrape off its scales, and don't stir it. If you do, it will turn to mush. Likewise, too much government makes those below rebel, and too much cultivation makes vitality wither."

HAN FEI says, "In cooking a small fish, too much turning ruins it. In governing a great state, too much reform embitters the people. Thus a ruler who possesses the Way values inaction over reform."

TE-CH'ING says, "A cruel government brings calamity down on the people. The people, though, think their suffering is the work of ghosts and spirits and turn to sacrifice and worship to improve their lot, when, actually, their misfortune is caused by their rulers."

THE TSOCHUAN says, "If the state is meant to flourish, listen to the people. If the state is meant to perish, listen to the spirits" (Chuang.32).

WANG CHEN says, "The government that takes peace as its basis doesn't lose the Way. When the government doesn't lose the Way, yin and yang are in harmony. When yin and yang are in harmony, wind and rain arrive on time. When wind and rain arrive on time, the spirit world is at peace. When the spirit world is at peace, the legion of demons can't perform their sorcery."

WANG PI says, "Spirits don't injure what is natural. What is natural gives spirits no opening. When spirits have no opening, spirits cannot act like spirits."

CH'ENG HSUAN-YING says, "Spirits dwell in the *yin,* and people dwell in the *yang.* When both accept their lot, neither injures the other."

SU CH'E says, "The inaction of the sage makes people content with the way they are. Outside, nothing troubles them. Inside, nothing frightens them. Even spirits have no means of using their powers. It isn't that spirits have no powers. They have powers, but they don't use them to harm people. The reason people and spirits don't harm each other is because they look up to the sage. And the sage never harms anyone."

WU CH'ENG says, "The reason spirits don't harm the people is not because they can't but because the sage is able to harmonize the energy of the people so that they don't injure the energy of the spirit world. The reason neither injures the other is due to the sage's virtue. Hence they both rely on the virtue of the sage."

HSUAN-TSUNG says, "'Neither' refers to spirits and the sage."

LI JUNG says, "Spirits and sages help others without harming each other. One is hidden, the other manifest. But both rely on virtue."

SUNG CH'ANG-HSING says, "Spirits are spirits because they respond but can't be seen. The sage is a sage because he governs but doesn't act. The virtue of the sage and the virtue of spirits is the same."

Commentators are divided as to whether the subjects of lines nine and ten are spirits and the people or spirits and the sage. Although both are possible, I prefer the latter interpretation.

61

大邦者下流。天下之交。天下之牝。牝恆以靜勝牡。為其靜。故宜為下。大邦以下小邦。則取小邦。小邦以下大邦。則取於大邦。故或下以取。或下而取。故大邦者不過欲。兼畜人。小邦者不過欲。入事人。夫皆得其欲。則大者宜為下。

The great state is a watershed
the confluence of the world
the female of the world
through stillness the female conquers the male
in order to be still
she needs to be lower
the great state that is lower
governs the small state
the small state that is lower
is governed by the great state
some lower themselves to govern
some lower themselves to be governed
the great state's only desire
is to unite and lead others
the small state's only desire
is to join and serve others
for both to achieve their desire
the greater needs to be lower

LAO-TZU says, "The reason the sea can govern a hundred rivers / is because it has mastered being lower" (66).

HO-SHANG KUNG says, "To lead a great state we should be like the sea: we should be at the bottom of a watershed and not fight even the smallest current. A great state is the meeting place of the high and the low. The female refers to everything *yin*: weak, humble, yielding, what doesn't lead."

TS'AO TAO-CH'UNG says, "The female is the mother. All creatures revere their mother. The sage recognizes the male but upholds the female. Hence all creatures turn to the sage."

SU CH'E says, "The world turns to a great state just as rivers flow downstream. If a great state can lower itself, small states will attach themselves to it. If a small state can lower itself, a great state will take it under its care. A great state lowers itself to govern others. A small state lowers itself to be governed by others."

WU CH'ENG says, "The female doesn't make the first move. It is always the male who makes the first move. But to move means to lose. To wait means to gain. To move means to be above. To wait means to be below. The great state that doesn't presume on its superiority gains the voluntary support of the small state. The small state that is content with its inferiority enjoys the generosity of the great state. The small state doesn't have to worry about being lower, while the great state does. Hence the great state needs to be lower."

WANG AN-SHIH says, "To serve someone greater is easy. To serve someone smaller is hard. Because it is hard, Lao-tzu says 'the greater needs to be lower.'"

MENCIUS says, "Only a virtuous ruler is able to serve a smaller state. Only a wise ruler is able to serve a greater state" (1B.3).

WANG PI says, "By cultivating humility, each gets what it wants. When the small state cultivates humility, it preserves itself, but that is all. It can't make the world turn to it. The world turns to the great state that cultivates humility. Thus each gets what it wants, but it is the great state that needs to be more humble."

The Fuyi edition adds *t'ien-hsia-chih:of the world* to line one, and the Mawangtui texts invert lines two and three. I have decided against both variants in favor of the standard edition. However, I have followed the Mawangtui texts in their wording of lines five and six. And I have followed them again, along with the Fuyi text, in their addition of the particle *yu:by* to line ten. This variant clarifies a relationship between great and small which was previously ambiguous and easily misinterpreted in the standard edition.

62

道者萬物之奧。善人之寶。不善人之所保。美言可以市。
尊行可以賀。人之不善。何棄之有。故立天子。置三卿
。雖有拱之璧。以先駟馬。不如坐。而進此道。古之所以
貴此者。何不謂。求以得。有罪以勉與。故為天下貴。

The Tao is creation's sanctuary
treasured by the good
it keeps the bad alive
beautiful words might be the price
noble deeds might be the gift
how can we abandon
people who are bad
thus when emperors are enthroned
or ministers installed
though there be great discs of jade
followed by teams of horses
they don't rival one who sits
and offers up this Way
why the ancients exalted it
did they not proclaim
who searches thereby finds
who errs thereby escapes
thus the world exalts it

THE HSISHENGCHING says, "The Tao is the sanctuary of the deepest depth and the source of empty nothingness."

WU CH'ENG says, "'Sanctuary' means the most honored place. The layout of ancestral shrines includes an outer hall and an inner chamber. The southwest corner of the inner chamber is called the 'sanctuary,' and the sanctuary is where the gods dwell."

SU CH'E says, "All we see of things is their outside, their entrance hall. The Tao is their sanctuary. We all have one, but we don't see it. The wise alone are able to find it. Hence Lao-tzu says the good treasure it. The foolish don't find it. But then, who doesn't the Tao protect? Hence he says it protects the bad. The Tao doesn't leave people. People leave the Tao."

124

WANG PI says, "Beautiful words can excel the products of the marketplace. Noble deeds can elicit a response a thousand miles away."

TE-CH'ING says, "The Tao is in us all. Though good and bad might differ, our natures are the same. How, then, can we abandon anyone?"

LAO-TZU says, "The sage is good at saving / yet he abandons no one / thus the good instruct the bad / the bad learn from the good" (27).

WANG P'ANG says, "Jade discs and fine horses are used to attract talented men to the government. But a government that finds talented men and does not implement the Tao is not followed by the people."

CHIANG HSI-CH'ANG says, "In ancient times, the less valuable presents came first, hence jade discs preceded horses."

LI HSI-CHAI says, "Better than discs of jade followed by teams of horses would be one good word or one good deed to keep the people from losing sight of the good."

LU NUNG-SHIH says, "If words and deeds can be offered to others, how much more the Tao."

WANG AN-SHIH says, "There is nothing that is not the Tao. When good people seek it, they are able to find it. When bad people seek it, they are able to avoid punishment."

In line one, both Mawangtui texts have *chu:flow/chief* instead of *ao:sanctuary*. But this destroys the rhyme in the following lines and is not supported by any other edition. In lines four and five, commentators have long suspected an error, and the Mawangtui texts have given us a partial solution. In line five, I have used their *ho-jen:give to people* in place of the standard *chia-jen:surpass people*. However, I have deleted *jen:people* as a copyist error for the word that begins the next line in Chinese. In my translation, I have inverted the order of the two lines that follow.

為無為。事無事。味無味。大小多少。報怨以德
。圖難於其易。為大於其細。天下之難作於易。
天下之大作於細。是以聖人終不為大。故能成其
大。夫輕諾必寡信。多易必多難。是以聖人猶
難之。故終於無難。

Act without acting
work without working
taste without tasting
great or small many or few
repay each wrong with virtue
plan for the hard while it's easy
work on the great while it's small
the hardest task in the world begins easy
the greatest goal in the world begins small
therefore the sage never acts great
he thus achieves great things
who quickly agrees is seldom trusted
who makes it all easy finds it all hard
therefore the sage makes everything hard
he thus finds nothing hard

HO-SHANG KUNG says, "To act without acting means to do only what is natural. To work without working means to avoid trouble by preparing in advance. To taste without tasting means to taste the meaning of the Tao through meditation."

LI HSI-CHAI says, "When we act without acting, we don't exhaust ourselves. When we work without working, we don't trouble others. When we taste without tasting, we don't waste anything."

WANG TAO says, "What people do involves action. What the sage does accords with the Tao of inaction. 'Work' refers to the conditions of action. 'Taste' refers to the meaning of action."

SUNG CH'ANG-HSING says, "To act without acting, to work without working, to taste without tasting is to conform with what is natural and not to impose oneself on others. Though others treat him wrongly, the wrong is theirs and not the sage's. He responds with the virtue within his heart. Utterly empty and detached, he thus moves others to trust in doing nothing."

126

CHIAO HUNG says, "Action involves form and thus includes great and small. It is also tied to number and thus includes many and few. This is where wrongs come from. Only the Tao is beyond form and beyond number. Thus the sage treats everything the same: great and small, many and few. Why should he respond to them with anger?"

TS'AO TAO-CH'UNG says, "If we repay wrongs with kindness, we put an end to revenge. If we repay wrongs with wrongs, revenge never ends."

HAN FEI says, "In terms of form, the great necessarily starts from the small. In terms of duration, the many necessarily starts from the few. The wise ruler detects small schemes and thus avoids great plots. He enacts minor punishments and thus avoids major rebellions."

DUKE WEN OF CHIN told KUO YEN, "In the beginning, I found it easy to rule the kingdom. Now I find it hard." Kuo Yen replied, "If you consider something easy, it is bound to become hard. If you consider something hard, it is bound to become easy" (*Kuoyu*: Chin.4).

WANG CHEN says, "If a ruler disdains something as easy, misfortune and trouble are sure to arise from it. If a ruler does not pay attention to small matters, eventually they will overwhelm even the greatest virtue. Thus the sage guards against the insignificant lest it amount to something great. If he waits until something is great before he acts, his action will come too late."

TE-CH'ING says, "When I entered the mountains to cultivate the Way, at first it was very hard. But once I learned how to use my mind, it became very easy. What the world considers hard, the sage considers easy. What the world considers easy, the sage considers hard."

In *Wentzu*: 1, line three appears as "know without knowing." But this variant occurs nowhere else. Lines ten and eleven also appear in verse 34.

64

其安易持。其未兆易謀。其脆易破。其微易散。為之於未有。治之於未亂。合抱之木生於毫末。九成之臺起於虆土。千里之行始於足下。為之者敗之。執之者失之。是以聖人無為。故無敗。無執。故無失。民之從事。恆於幾成而敗之。慎終如始。則無敗事矣。是以聖人欲不欲。而不貴難得之貨。學不學。而復眾人之所過。以輔萬物之自然。而不敢為。

It's easy to rule while it's peaceful
it's easy to plan before it arrives
it's easy to break while it's fragile
it's easy to disperse while it's small
act before it exists
govern before it rebels
a giant tree grows from the tiniest shoot
a great tower rises from a basket of dirt
a thousand-mile journey begins at your feet
but to act is to fail
to control is to lose
therefore the sage doesn't act
he thus doesn't fail
he doesn't control
he thus doesn't lose
when people pursue a task
they always fail near the end
care at the end as well as the start
means an end to failure
the sage thus seeks what no one seeks
he doesn't prize hard-to-get goods
he studies what no one studies
he turns to what others pass by
to help all things be natural
he thus dares not act

LU HUI-CH'ING says, "We should act before things exist, while they are peaceful and latent. We should govern before they rebel, while they are fragile and small. But to act before things exist means to act without acting. To govern before things rebel means to govern without governing."

SU CH'E says, "To act before things exist comes first. To govern before they rebel comes next."

KUAN-TZU says, "Know where gain and loss lie, then act" (47).

HUAI-NAN-TZU says, "A needle makes a tapestry. A basket of earth makes a wall. Success and failure begin from something small" (16).

SUNG CH'ANG-HSING says, "From a sprout, the small becomes great. From a basket of earth, the low becomes high. From here, the near becomes far. But trees are cut down, towers are toppled, and journeys end. Everything we do eventually results in failure. Everything we control is eventually lost. But if we act before things exist, how can we fail? If we govern before they rebel, how can we lose?"

WANG P'ANG says, "Everything has its course. When the time is right, it arrives. But people are blind to this truth and work to speed things up. They try to help Heaven and end up ruining things just as they near completion."

HO-SHANG KUNG says, "Others seek the ornamental. The sage seeks the simple. Others seek form. The sage seeks Virtue. Others study facts and skills. The sage studies what is natural. Others study how to govern the world. The sage studies how to govern himself and how to uphold the truth of the Way."

HAN FEI says, "The wise don't fill their lessons with words or their shelves with books. The world may pass them by, but the ruler turns to them when he wants to study what no one studies."

WU CH'ENG says, "The sage seeks without seeking and studies without studying. For the truth of all things lies not in acting but in doing what is natural. By not acting, the sage shares in the naturalness of all things."

For line nine, the Mawangtui texts have: "a height of a hundred fathoms."

65

古之善為道者。非以明民。將以愚之。民之難治。以
其智。故以智治邦。邦之賊。不以智治邦。邦之德
。恆知此兩者。亦稽式。恆知稽式。是謂玄德。玄
德深矣。遠矣。與物反矣。乃至大順。

The ancient masters of the Way
tried not to enlighten
but to keep men in the dark
what makes the people hard to rule
is knowledge
who rules the realm with knowledge
spreads evil in the realm
who rules without knowledge
spreads virtue in the realm
who understands these two
understands the universal key
understanding the universal key
this is called Dark Virtue
Dark Virtue goes deep
goes far
goes the other way
until it reaches perfect harmony

WU CH'ENG says, "To make the people more natural, the ancient sages did not try to make the people more knowledgeable but to make them less knowledgeable. This radical doctrine was later misused by the First Emperor of the Ch'in dynasty, who burned all the books (in 213 BC) to make the people ignorant."

CHUANG-TZU says, "When the knowledge of bows and arrows arose, the birds above were troubled. When the knowledge of hooks and nets proliferated, the fish below were disturbed. When the knowledge of snares and traps spread, the creatures of the wild were bewildered. When the knowledge of argument and disputation multiplied, the people were confused. Thus are the world's troubles due to the love of knowledge" (10.4).

WANG PI says, "When you rouse the people with sophistry, treacherous thoughts arise. When you counter their deceptions with more sophistry, the people see through your tricks and avoid them. Thus they become secretive and devious."

LIU CHUNG-P'ING says, "Those who rule without knowledge turn to Heaven. Those who rule with knowledge turn to Man. Those who turn to Heaven are in harmony. Those who are in harmony do only what requires no effort. Their government is lenient. Those who turn to Man force things. Those who force things become lost in the Great Inquisition. Hence their people are dishonest." Liu's terminology here is indebted to *Chuangtzu: 19.2* and *Mencius: 4B.26*.

HO-SHANG KUNG says, "'Two' refers to 'knowledge' and 'without knowledge.' Once you know that knowledge spreads evil and lack of knowledge spreads virtue, you understand the key to cultivating the self and governing the realm. Once you understand the key, you share the same virtue as Heaven. And Heaven is dark. Those who possess Dark Virtue are so deep they can't be fathomed, so distant they can't be reached, and are always doing the opposite of others. They give to others, while others think only of themselves."

SUNG CH'ANG-HSING says, "Because it is so deep, you can't hear it or see it. Because it is so far, you can't talk about it or reach it. Dark Virtue differs from everything else, but it agrees with the Tao."

SU CH'E says, "What the sage values is virtue. What others value is knowledge. Virtue and knowledge are opposites. Knowledge is seldom harmonious, while virtue is always in harmony."

LIN HSI-YI says, "'Perfect harmony' is whatever is natural."

Line one also begins verse 15. I have followed the Mawangtui texts in line six, where they omit *to:too much*, and also in line nine, where they replace *fu:blessing* with *te:virtue*. This last variant also appears in *Wentzu: 1*.

66

江海之所以能為百谷王。以其善下之。故能為百
谷王。是以聖人之欲上民也。必以其言下之。其
欲先民也。必以其身後之。是以聖人居上。而
民不重。居前。而民不害。天下皆樂推。而不
厭。以其不爭。故天下莫能與之爭。

The reason the sea can govern a hundred rivers

is because it has mastered being lower

thus it can govern a hundred rivers

thus if the sage would be above the people

he should speak as if he were below them

if he would be before them

he should act as if he were behind them

thus when the sage is above

the people are not burdened

when he is in front

the people are not hindered

the world never wearies

of pushing him forward

because he doesn't struggle

no one can struggle against him

YEN TSUN says, "Rivers don't flow toward the sea because of its reputation or its power, but because it does nothing and seeks nothing."

TE-CH'ING says, "All rivers flow toward the sea, regardless of whether they are muddy or clear. And the sea is able to contain them all because it is adept at staying below them. This is a metaphor for the sage. The world turns to him because he is selfless."

LU HUI-CH'ING says, "When the sage possesses the kingdom, he speaks of himself as 'orphaned, widowed, and impoverished,' or 'inheritor of the country's shame and misfortune.' Thus in his speech, he places himself below others. He does not act unless he is forced. He does not respond unless he is moved. He does not rise unless he has no choice. Thus in his actions, he places himself behind others."

HO-SHANG KUNG says, "When the sage rules over the people, he doesn't oppress those below with his position. Thus the people uphold him and don't think of him as a burden. When he stands before them, he doesn't blind them with his glory. Thus the people love him as a parent and harbor no resentment. The sage is kind and loving and treats the people as if they were his children. Thus the whole world wants him for their leader. The people never grow tired of him because he doesn't struggle against them. Everyone struggles against something. But no one struggles against a person who doesn't struggle against anything."

SU CH'E says, "The sage doesn't try to be above or in front of others. But when he finds himself below or behind others, the Tao can't help but lift him up and push him forward."

YANG HSIUNG says, "He who holds himself back is advanced by others. He who lowers himself is lifted up by others" (*Fayen:* 7).

LI HSI-CHAI says, "The people aren't burdened when the sage is above them, because they aren't aware they have a ruler. And the people aren't hindered when the sage is before them, because he isn't aware they are his people."

WANG CHEN says, "Through humility the sage gains the approval of the people. Once he gains their approval, he gains their tireless support. And once he gains their tireless support, struggling over rank naturally comes to an end."

There is a relative lack of commentary for this verse. Wang Pi, for example, says nothing at all. The only textual issue is whether to read the last two lines as a statement or as a rhetorical question ("Is it not because he doesn't struggle / no one can struggle against him?"). The Mawangtui and Fuyi texts word them as a question, while the Suotan and standard versions, which I have followed, word them as a statement. Both lines also appear as a statement in verse 22.

67

天下皆謂我大。大而不肖。夫唯大故不肖。若肖。久矣其細。夫我恆有三寶

。持而寶之。一曰慈。二曰儉。三曰不敢為天下先。夫慈。故能勇。儉。故

能廣。不敢為天下先。故能為成器長。今捨其慈且勇。捨其儉且廣。捨其後

且先。則死矣。夫慈以戰則勝。以守

則固。天將建之。以慈垣之。

The world calls me great

great but useless

because I am great I am useless

if I were of use

I would have stayed small

but I possess three treasures

I treasure and uphold

first is compassion

second is austerity

third is reluctance to excel

because I am compassionate

I can be valiant

because I am austere

I can be extravagant

because I am reluctant to excel

I can be chief of all tools

if I renounced compassion for valor

austerity for extravagance

reluctance for supremacy

I would die

compassion wins every battle

and outlasts every attack

what Heaven creates

let compassion protect

HO-SHANG KUNG says, "Lao-tzu says the world calls his virtue great. But if his virtue were great in name alone it would bring him harm. Hence he acts stupid and useless. He doesn't distinguish or differentiate. Nor does he demean others or glorify himself."

WANG PI says, "To be useful is to lose the means to be great."

SU CH'E says, "The world honors daring, exalts ostentation, and emphasizes progress. What the sage treasures is patience, frugality, and humility, all of which the world considers useless."

TE-CH'ING says, "'Compassion' means to embrace all creatures without reservation. 'Austerity' means not to exhaust what one already has. 'Reluctance to excel' means to drift through the world without opposing others."

WANG AN-SHIH says, "Through compassion, we learn to be soft. When we are soft, we can overcome the hardest thing in the world. Thus we can be valiant. Through austerity, we learn when to stop. When we know when to stop, we are always content. Thus we can be extravagant. Through reluctance to excel, we are excelled by no one. Thus we can be chief of all tools. Valor, extravagance, and excellence are what everyone worries about. And because they worry, they are always on the verge of death."

LIU SHIH-P'EI says, "To be chief of all tools means to be the chief official." For "chief of all tools," see verse 28.

CONFUCIUS says, "The gentleman is not a tool" (*Lunyu:* 2.12).

WU CH'ENG says, "Compassion is the chief of the three treasures. The last section only mentions compassion because it includes the other two. All people love a compassionate person as they do their own parents. How could anyone oppose their parents? Hence he who attacks or defends with compassion meets no opposition."

MENCIUS says, "He who is kind has no enemy under Heaven" (7B.3).

Several editions read line one: "The world calls my Tao great." But the word *Tao* does not appear in the Fuyi or Suotan editions, the Mawangtui texts, or in other early copies. In line sixteen, Han Fei and Mawangtui Text A have *ch'eng-shih-chang:chief of those who succeed*. For the penultimate line, I have followed the Mawangtui version, which has *chien:create* instead of the standard *chiu:save*.

68

古之極。
是謂用人之力。是謂配天
人者為之下。是謂不爭之德
不怒。善勝敵者不與。善用
古之。善為士者不武。善戰者

In ancient times

the perfect officer wasn't armed

the perfect warrior wasn't angry

the perfect victor wasn't hostile

the perfect commander acted humble

this is the virtue of nonaggression

this is using the strength of others

this is uniting with Heaven

which was the ancient end

CHIAO HUNG says, "In ancient times, officers went to battle in chariots. They were dressed in mail, and there were three to a vehicle: one on the left armed with a bow, one on the right armed with a spear, and one in the middle in charge of the reins, the flag, and the drum. Below and arrayed around every chariot were seventy-two soldiers."

SUN-TZU says, "A ruler must not mobilize his armies in anger. A general must not engage the enemy in wrath. Anger can turn to joy, and wrath can turn to gladness. But once a state is destroyed, it cannot be restored. And once a man is dead, he cannot be reborn" (12.18–21). Sun-tzu also says, "To win every battle is not supreme excellence. Supreme excellence is to conquer without fighting" (3.2).

HO-SHANG KUNG says, "Those who honor the Way and Virtue are not fond of weapons. They keep hatred from their hearts. They eliminate disaster before it arises. They are angered by nothing. They use kindness among neighbors and virtue among strangers. And they conquer their enemies without fighting. They commmand through humility."

LIEH-TZU says, "He who governs others with worthiness never wins them over. He who serves them with worthiness never fails to gain their support" (6.3).

WANG CHEN says, "You must first win their hearts before you can command others."

KUMARAJIVA says, "Empty your body and mind. No one can fight against nothing."

WU CH'ENG says, "Even though our wisdom and power might surpass that of others, we should act as if we possessed neither. By making ourselves lower than others, we can use their wisdom and power as our own. Thus we can win without taking up arms, without getting angry, and without making enemies. By using the virtue of nonagression and the power of others, we are like Heaven, which overcomes without fighting and reaches its goal without moving."

TZU-SSU says, "Wide and deep, he is able to support others. High and bright, he is able to protect others. He who is wide and deep unites with Earth. He who is high and bright unites with Heaven" (*Chungyung*: 26.4–5).

TE-CH'ING says, "Heaven is *yang* and Earth is *yin*. But if Heaven and Earth remain stationary, everything stops, and nothing comes into existence. Only when *yang* descends and *yin* rises does everything flourish. Thus Heaven's position is to be above, but its function is to descend. When the sage is above the people, and his heart is below, we call this uniting with Heaven. This was the pole star of the ancient kings."

Some editions drop the opening phrase: *ku-chih:in ancient times* and combine this with the previous verse. I have followed the Fuyi edition in retaining it as it stands (Mawangtui Text B has *ku:thus*). In line seven, both Mawangtui texts omit the phrase: *chih-li:the strength of,* but no other edition follows suit. Finally, some commentators read the last two lines as one line, eliminating *ku:ancient* as a copyist error: "we call this the end of uniting with Heaven." But this is not supported by any early commentary or text.

69

用兵有言曰。吾不敢為主。而為客。不
敢進寸。而退尺。是謂行無行。攘無臂
。執無兵。扔無敵。禍莫大於無敵。無
敵近亡吾寶。故抗兵相若。則哀者勝矣。

In warfare there is a saying
rather than a host
better to be a guest
rather than advance an inch
better to retreat a foot
this means to form no column
to wear no armor
to brandish no weapon
to repulse no enemy
no fate is worse than to have no enemy
without an enemy we would lose our treasure
thus when opponents are evenly matched
the remorseful one prevails

WANG CHEN says, "In warfare, we say the one who mobilizes first is the host and the one who responds is the guest. The sage only goes to war when he has no choice. Hence he is the guest."

CHIAO HUNG says, "This was a saying of ancient military strategists." If so, they remain unnamed. Sun-tzu, meanwhile, calls the invading force the *k'o:guest* (II.20).

HO-SHANG KUNG says, "According to the Tao of warfare, we should avoid being the first to mobilize troops, and we should go to war only after receiving Heaven's blessing."

LU HUI-CH'ING says, "The host resists, and the guest agrees. The host toils, and the guest relaxes. One advances with pride, while the other retreats in humility. One advances with action, while the other retreats in quiet. He who meets resistance with agreement, toil with relaxation, pride with humility, and action with quiet has no enemy. Wherever he goes, he conquers."

SUNG CH'ANG-HSING says, "In warfare, the sage leaves no traces. He advances by retreating."

WU CH'ENG says, "Those who go to war form themselves into columns, equip themselves with weapons, and advance against the enemy. But when the sage goes to war, he acts as if columns did not exist, armor did not exist, weapons did not exist, as if enemies did not exist."

SUN-TZU says, "The general who advances with no thought of fame, who retreats with no fear of punishment, who thinks only of protecting his country and helping his king is the treasure of the realm" (10.24).

SU CH'E says, "The sage regards compassion as his treasure. To treat killing lightly would be to lose the reason for compassion."

TE-CH'ING says, "When opponents are evenly matched, and neither is superior, the winner is hard to determine. But if one is remorseful and compassionate, he will win. For the Way of Heaven is to love life and to help those who are compassionate to overcome their enemies."

WANG PI says, "Those who are remorseful sympathize with their opponents. They don't try to gain an advantage but to avoid injury. Hence they always win."

WANG P'ANG says, "To be remorseful is to be compassionate. He who is compassionate is able to be courageous. Thus he triumphs."

LIN HSI-YI says, "Those who attack with drums and cheer the advent of war are not remorseful. They are remorseful who do not consider warfare a pleasure but an occasion for mourning. In this verse, warfare is only a metaphor for the Tao."

LAO-TZU says, "When you kill another / honor him with your tears / when the battle is won / treat it as a wake" (31).

The standard edition reverses lines eight and nine. In lines ten and eleven, it also has *ch'ing-ti:treat enemies lightly* in place of *wu-ti:without enemies.* And in line twelve, it has *hsiang-chia:meet each other* in place of *hsiang-juo:evenly matched.* In all three cases, I have followed the Mawangtui and Fuyi editions.

70

吾言甚易知。其易行。而人莫之能知
。莫之能行。言有宗。事有君。夫唯
無知。是以不我知。知我者希。則我
貴矣。是以聖人被褐。而懷玉。

My words are easy to understand

easy to employ

but no one can understand them

no one can employ them

words have an ancestor

deeds have a master

because they have no understanding

people fail to understand me

rare are they who understand me

thus am I exalted

the sage therefore wears coarse cloth

and keeps his jade inside

TS'AO TAO-CH'UNG says, "Nothing is simpler or easier than the Tao. But because it's so simple, it can't be explained by reasoning. Hence no one can understand it. And because it's so near, it can't be reached by stages. Hence no one can put it to use."

WANG P'ANG says, "Because the sage teaches us to be in harmony with the course of our life, his words are simple, and his deeds are ordinary. Those who look within themselves understand. Those who follow their own nature do what is right. Difficulties arise when we turn away from the trunk and follow the branches."

LI HSI-CHAI says, "The Tao is easy to understand and easy to put to use. It is also hard to understand and hard to put to use. It is easy because there is no Tao to discuss, no knowledge to learn, no effort to make, no deeds to perform. And it is hard because the Tao cannot be discussed, because all words are wrong, because it cannot be learned, and because the mind only leads us astray. Effortless stillness is not necessarily right. And actionless activity is not necessarily wrong. This is why it is hard."

SU CH'E says, "Words can trap the Tao, and deeds can reveal its signs. But if the Tao could be found in words, we would only have to listen to words. And if it could be seen in deeds, we would only have to examine deeds. But it cannot be found in words or seen in deeds. Only if we put aside words and look for their ancestor, put aside deeds and look for their master, can we find it."

WU CH'ENG says, "The ancestor unites the clan. The master governs the state. Softness and humility are the ancestor of all words and the master of all deeds."

YEN TSUN says, "Wild geese fly for days but don't know what exists beyond the sky. Officials and scholars work for years, but none of them knows the extent of the Way. It's beyond the ken and beyond the reach of narrow-minded, one-sided people."

LU HUI-CH'ING says, "The reason the Tao is exalted by the world is because it cannot be known or perceived. If it could be known or perceived why should it be exalted? Hence Lao-tzu is exalted because so few understand him. Thus the sage wears an embarrassed, foolish expression and seldom shows anyone his great and noble virtue."

HO-SHANG KUNG says, "The reason people don't understand me is because my virtue is dark and not visible from the outside."

CONFUCIUS says, "I study what is below and understand what is above. Who knows me? Only Heaven" (*Lunyu*: 14.37).

WANG PI says, "To wear coarse cloth is to become one with the mundane. To keep one's jade inside is to treasure the truth. The sage is difficult to know because he does not differ from the mundane and because he does not reveal his treasure of jade."

In line ten, the word *tse:thus* can also mean *follow*, and some commentators have read the line: "who follows me is exalted." As with geodes, jade is found inside ordinary-looking rocks. Officials once wore it on their hats as an emblem of their status, and alchemists often included it in their elixirs.

71

知不知。尚矣。不知
知。病矣。是以聖
人之不病。以其病
病。是以不病。

To understand yet not understand
is transcendence
not to understand yet understand
is affliction
the reason the sage is not afflicted
is because he treats affliction as affliction
hence he is not afflicted

CONFUCIUS says, "Shall I teach you about understanding? To treat understanding as understanding and to treat not understanding as not understanding, this is understanding" (*Lunyu:* 2.17).

TE-CH'ING says, "The ancients said that the word 'understanding' was the door to all mysteries as well as the door to all misfortune. If you realize that you don't understand, you eliminate false understanding. This is the door to all mysteries. If you cling to understanding while trying to discover what you don't understand, you increase the obstacles to understanding. This is the door to all misfortune."

WU CH'ENG says, "Those who understand yet who seem not to understand are the wisest of men. They protect their understanding with stupidity. Those who don't understand yet who think they understand are, in fact, the stupidest of men. They think blind eyes see and deaf ears hear. This is what is meant by 'affliction.'"

TS'AO TAO-CH'UNG says, "If someone understands, but out of humility he says he doesn't understand, this is when reality is superior to name. Hence we call it transcendence. If someone doesn't understand but says he does understand, this is when name surpasses reality. Hence we call this an affliction. Those who are able to understand that affliction is affliction are never afflicted."

SU CH'E says, "The Tao is not something that can be reached through reasoning. Hence it cannot be understood. Those who do not yet understand do not understand that there is no entrance. And if they do understand, and they think about their understanding, they become afflicted by understanding."

CHIAO HUNG says, "Anything that is understood is a delusion. Anything that is a delusion is an affliction. Understanding is not the affliction. It is the understanding of understanding that becomes the affliction. To understand what is the affliction is to cure the illness without medicine."

LI HSI-CHAI says, "Understanding depends on things, hence it involves fabrication. Not understanding returns to the origin, hence it approaches the truth. If someone can understand that not understanding approaches the truth and that understanding involves fabrication, they are transcendent. If they don't understand that understanding involves fabrication and vainly increase their understanding, they use the affliction as the medicine. Only by understanding that understanding is affliction can one be free of affliction. This is why the sage is not afflicted."

HO-SHANG KUNG says, "To understand the Tao yet to say that we don't is the transcendence of virtue. Not to understand the Tao and to say that we do is the affliction of virtue. Lesser people don't understand the meaning of the Tao and vainly act according to their forced understanding and thereby harm their spirit and shorten their years. The sage doesn't suffer the affliction of forced understanding because he is pained by the affliction of others."

The Fuyi and standard editions include two additional lines between lines four and five: "because he treats affliction as affliction / he is not afflicted." But this makes the last lines more redundant than they already are, and they are not included by Han Fei, the Mawangtui texts, the Chinglung edition, or at least two Tunhuang copies.

72

民之不畏畏。則大畏將之矣。勿
狹其所居。勿厭其所生。夫唯弗厭
。是以不厭。是以聖人自知。而不
自見。自愛。而不自貴。故去彼
而取此。

When people no longer fear authority
a greater authority will appear
don't restrict where people dwell
don't repress how people live
if they aren't repressed
they won't protest
thus the sage knows himself
but doesn't reveal himself
he loves himself
but doesn't exalt himself
thus he picks this over that

WU CH'ENG says, "The authority we fear is what shortens years and takes lives. The 'greater authority' is our greater fear, namely death. When people no longer fear what they ought to fear, they advance their own death until the greater fear appears."

WANG P'ANG says, "When people are simple and their lives are good, they fear authority. But when those above lose the Way and enact all sorts of measures to restrict the livelihood of those below, people respond with deceit and are no longer subdued by authority. When this happens, natural calamities occur and misfortunes arise."

WANG CHEN says, "When ordinary officials and the common people have no fear, punishment occurs. When ministers and high officials have no fear, banishment occurs. When princes and kings have no fear, warfare occurs."

WEI YUAN says, "'Where they dwell' refers to conditions such as wealth and poverty. 'How they live' refers to bodily activities such as toil and rest. When people think that where they dwell or how they live is not as good as others, they feel embarrassed and thus restricted, restricted and thus repressed. And when they feel repressed, they protest against 'this' and seek 'that,' not knowing that once their desire is fulfilled what they fear comes close behind."

WANG PI says, "In tranquility and peace is where we should dwell. Humble and empty is how we should live. But when we forsake tranquility to pursue desires and abandon humility for authority, creatures are disturbed and people are distressed. When authority cannot restore order, and people cannot endure authority, the link between those above and those below is severed, and natural calamities occur."

HO-SHANG KUNG says, "He knows what he has and what he doesn't have. He doesn't display his virtue outside but keeps it hidden inside. He loves his body and protects his essence and breath. He doesn't exalt or glorify himself before the world. 'That' refers to showing and glorifying himself. 'This' refers to knowing and loving himself."

TS'AO TAO-CH'UNG says, "'That' refers to external things. 'This' refers to one's inner reality."

Lao-tzu begins this verse with two puns. The force of the first pun in lines one and two is somewhat weakened in the standard edition by the use of homophones for "fear" and "authority." In his edition of 1587, Chiao Hung noted that in ancient times these words were interchangeable, and he suggested using one character for both words. This is, in fact, what occurs in the second pun in lines five and six, where the same character is used for "repress" as well as for "protest." The Mawangtui texts, it turns out, agree with Chiao Hung, and I have amended lines one and two accordingly. In lines three and four, I have also turned to the Mawangtui texts for the negative injunction *wu:don't*. Other editions have *wu:has not* or *pu:does not*, both of which result in problems regarding the referant and thus different interpretations of the entire verse. The last line also occurs at the end of verses 12 and 38.

73

勇於敢則殺。勇於不敢則活。此兩者。或利
。或害。天之所惡。孰知其故。天之道。不
爭而善勝。不言而善應。不召而自來。繟而
善謀。天網恢恢。疏而不失。

Daring to act means death
daring not to act means life
of these two
one benefits
one harms
what Heaven hates
who knows the reason
the Way of Heaven
wins easily without a fight
answers wisely without a word
comes quickly without a summons
plans ingeniously without a thought
the Net of Heaven is all-embracing
its mesh is wide but nothing escapes

LI HSI-CHAI says, "Everyone knows about daring to act but not about daring not to act. Those who dare to act walk on the edge of a knife. Those who dare not to act walk down the middle of the path. Comparing these two, walking on a knife-edge is harmful, but people ignore the harm. Walking down the middle of the path is beneficial, but people are not aware of the benefit. Thus it is said, 'People can walk on the edge of a knife but not down the middle of a path'" (Chungyung: 9).

SU CH'E says, "Those who dare to act die. Those who dare not to act live. This is the normal pattern of things. But sometimes those who act live, and sometimes those who don't act die. What happens in the world depends on luck. Sometimes what should happen doesn't. The Way of Heaven is far-off. Who knows where its love and hate come from?"

SUNG CH'ANG-HSING says, "The mechanism whereby some live and others die is obscure and hard to fathom. If the sage finds it difficult to know, what about ordinary people?"

YEN TSUN says, "Heaven does not consider life in its schemes or death in its work. It is impartial."

LU NUNG-SHIH says, "Loosely viewed, the hard and the strong conquer the soft and the weak. Correctly viewed, the soft and the weak conquer the hard and the strong. Hence the hard and the strong are what Heaven hates."

WU CH'ENG says, "Because the sage does not lightly kill others, evildoers slip through his net, but not the Net of Heaven. Heaven does not use its strength to fight against evildoers as Man does, and yet it always triumphs. It does not speak with a mouth as Man does, and yet it answers faster than an echo. It does not have to be summoned but arrives on its own. Evil has its evil reward. Even the clever cannot escape. Heaven is unconcerned and unmindful, but its retribution is ingenious and beyond the reach of human plans. It never lets an evildoer slip through its net. The sage does not have to kill him. Heaven will do it for him."

WANG AN-SHIH says, "*Yin* and *yang* take turns, the four seasons come and go, the moon waxes and wanes. All things have their time. They don't have to be summoned to come."

LI HUNG-FU says, "It wins because it doesn't fight. It answers because it doesn't speak. It comes because it isn't summoned. If it had to fight to win, something would escape, even if its mesh were fine."

After line seven, the Fuyi, Suotan, and standard editions have: "thus even the sage finds it hard." However, this line does not appear in the Mawangtui, Chinglung, or Suichou editions, Tunhuang copies P.2347, P.2517, S.6453, or the Yen Tsun text. Ma Hsu-lun considers it an interpolation from verse 63, where it also appears, and I tend to agree. The last two lines have become a proverb.

74

若民恆不畏死。奈何以殺懼之。若
使民恆畏死。而為奇者。吾將得而
殺之。夫孰敢矣。若民恆必畏死。則
恆有司殺者。夫代司殺者殺。是代大
匠斲。夫代大匠斲。則希有不傷其手。

If people no longer fear death
why do we threaten to kill them
and if others fear death
and still act perverse
and we catch and kill them
who else will dare
as long as people fear death
the executioner will exist
to kill in the executioner's place
is to take the carpenter's place
who takes the carpenter's place
is bound to hurt his hands

YIN WEN says, "Lao-tzu says if people are not afraid to die, what good is threatening to kill them? If people are not afraid to die, it is because punishments are excessive. When punishments are excessive, people don't care about life. When they don't care about life, the ruler's might means nothing to them. When punishments are moderate, people are afraid to die. They are afraid to die because they enjoy life. When you know they enjoy life, you can threaten them with death" (2).

LI HSI-CHAI says, "This implies that punishments cannot be relied upon for governing. If people are not afraid of death, what use is threatening them with execution? And if they are afraid of death, and we catch someone who breaks the law, and we execute them, by killing one person we should be able to govern the rest. But the more people we kill, the more break the law. Thus punishment is not the answer."

MING T'AI-TSU says, "When I first ascended the throne, the people were unruly and officials corrupt. If ten people were executed in the morning, a hundred were breaking the same law by evening. Being ignorant of the Way of the ancient sage kings, I turned to the *Taoteching*. When I read: 'If the people no longer fear death / why do we threaten to kill them,' I decided to do away with capital punishment and put criminals to work instead. In the year since then, the burdens of my heart have been lightened. Truly, this book is the greatest teacher of kings."

WU CH'ENG says, "'Perverse' means 'unlawful.' If those who act perverse and break the law do not meet with misfortune at the hands of Man, they will certainly be punished by Heaven."

HO-SHANG KUNG says, "If the ruler teaches according to the Tao, and people respond with perversion instead, the ruler is within his rights to arrest them and kill them. Lao-tzu, however, was concerned that the ruler should use the Tao first before he turned to punishment."

LU HUI-CH'ING says, "The meaning of 'the executioner will exist' is the same as 'the Net of Heaven is all-embracing / its mesh is wide but nothing escapes' (verse 73). The executioner is Heaven."

SU CH'E says, "Heaven is the executioner. If the world is at peace and someone engages in perversity and rebellion, then surely he has been abandoned by Heaven. If we kill him, it is Heaven who kills him and not us. But if we kill those whom Heaven has not abandoned, this is to take the executioner's place. And he who takes the executioner's place puts himself within reach of the axe."

THE LUSHIH CHUNCHIU says, "A great carpenter does not cut" (1.4).

MENCIUS says, "The wise are not alone in desiring something greater than life and in hating something greater than death. This is true of everyone. But the wise don't forget it" (6A.10).

Line seven appears only in the Mawangtui texts, but it seems needed to complete the meaning of line eight. At the end of line eight, the Fuyi and standard editions add an extra *sha:to kill*. I have followed the Suotan, Chingfu, and Mawangtui texts in omitting it.

民之飢。以其上食稅之多。是以飢。民之難治。以其上之有為。是以難治。民之輕死。以其上求生之厚。是以輕死。夫唯無以生為者。是賢於貴生。

The reason the people are hungry
is because those above levy so many taxes
thus the people are hungry
the reason the people are hard to rule
is because those above are so forceful
thus the people are hard to rule
the reason the people think little of death
is because those above think so much of life
thus the people think little of death
meanwhile those who do nothing to live
are more esteemed than those who love life

75

DUKE AI approached YU JUO, "The year is one of famine, and my revenues are wanting. What am I to do?" Yu Juo replied, "Return to the 10 percent rate of taxation." Duke Ai said, "But I cannot get by on 20 percent, how will I survive on 10 percent?" Yu Juo replied, "When the people do not want, why should the ruler want. When the people want, why should the ruler not want?" (*Lunyu*: 12.9).

WANG PI says, "The reason the people hide and disorder prevails is because of those above, not because of those below. The people follow those above."

LI HSI-CHAI says, "If those above take too much, those below will be impoverished. If those above use too much force, those below will rebel. This is a matter of course. When someone thinks his own life is more important, and he disregards the lives of others, why should others not treat death lightly. The sage doesn't think about life unless he is forced to."

TE-CH'ING says, "Robbers and thieves arise from hunger and cold. If people are hungry and have no means to live, they have no choice but to steal. When people steal, it's because those above force them. They force people to turn to stealing and then try to rule them with cleverness and laws. But the more laws they make, the more thieves appear. Even the threat of the executioner's axe doesn't frighten them. And the reason the people aren't frightened by death is because those above are so concerned with life."

SU CH'E says, "When those above use force to lead the people, the people respond with force. Thus do complications multiply, and the people become hard to rule."

WANG CHEN says, "'Forceful' refers to the ruler's love of might and arms. But once arms prevail, disorder is certain."

HUAI-NAN-TZU says, "The reason people cannot live out their alloted years and are sentenced to death in mid-life is because they think so much of life. Meanwhile, those who do nothing to stay alive are able to lengthen their lives" (7).

HO-SHANG KUNG says, "Only those who do nothing to stay alive, who aren't moved by titles or sinecures, who aren't affected by wealth or advantages, who refuse to serve the emperor or run errands for lesser lords, they alone are more esteemed than those who love life."

YEN TSUN says, "The Natural Way always turns things upside down. What has no body lives. What has a body dies. To be alive and to seek advantages is the beginning of death. Not to be alive and to get rid of advantages is the beginning of life. Those who don't work to live live long."

WANG TAO says, "The meaning of the last two lines is: If I didn't have this body of mine, what worries would I have?"

WANG P'ANG says, "If you understand only one of these three, you can understand the other two."

In line eight, I have followed the Fuyi edition in reading *ch'i-shang:those above.* Other editions have simply *ch'i:those,* leaving the referent in doubt.

76

人之生也。柔弱。其死也。堅強。草木之生也。柔脆。其死也。枯槁。故曰。堅強者死之徒也。柔弱者生之徒也。兵強則滅。木強則折。堅強居下。柔弱居上。

When people are born
they are soft and supple
when they perish
they are hard and stiff
when plants shoot forth
they are soft and tender
when they die
they are withered and dry
thus it is said
the hard and strong are followers of death
the soft and weak are followers of life
when an army becomes strong it suffers defeat
when a plant becomes hard it snaps
the hard and strong dwell below
the soft and weak dwell above

HO-SHANG KUNG says, "When people are born, they contain breath and spirit. This is why they are soft. When they die, their breath ceases and their spirit disappears. This is why they are hard."

WU CH'ENG says, "Seeing that the living are soft and the dead are hard, we can infer that those whose virtue is hard and those whose actions are forceful die before they are ready, while those who are soft and weak are able to preserve their lives."

LI HSI-CHAI says, "Although the soft and weak aren't the same as the Tao, they approach its absence of effort. Hence they aren't far from the Tao. Although the hard and strong aren't outside the Tao, they involve effort. Hence they lead people away from it."

LIEH-TZU says, "The world has a path of perennial victory and a path of perennial defeat. The path of perennial victory is weakness. The path of perennial defeat is strength. These two are easy to recognize, but people remain oblivious to them" (2.17).

LAO-TZU says, "The weak conquer the strong" (36).

WANG CHEN says, "It isn't hard for an army to achieve victory. But it is hard to hold onto victory. There is no great army that has not brought on its own defeat through its victories."

HSI T'UNG says, "When wood becomes hard, it loses its flexibility and becomes easy to break."

WANG P'ANG says, "In terms of yin and yang, yin comes before, and yang comes after. In terms of Heaven and Earth, Heaven is exalted, and Earth is humble. In terms of Virtue, the soft and the weak overcome the hard and the strong. But in terms of material things, the hard and the strong control the soft and the weak. The people of this world only see things. They don't understand Virtue."

SU CH'E says, "As long as it contains empty breath, the body does not suffer from rigidity. As long as they reflect perfect reason, actions are not burdened by severity. According to the unchanging principle of things, the refined rises to the top, while the coarse sinks to the bottom. The refined is soft and weak, while the coarse is hard and strong."

LI JUNG says, "The living belong above. The dead belong below."

In line five, most editions include the phrase *wan-wu:ten thousand creatures* before *ts'ao-wu:plants.* Chiang Hsi-ch'ang thinks that in light of the plant-specific adjectives of lines six and eight this must be an interpolation, and I agree. It does not appear in Yen Tsun or the Fuyi edition. In line nine, I have relied on the Mawangtui texts for the addition of *yueh:it is said.* In line thirteen, I have turned to *Liehtzu:* 2.17, *Huainantzu:* 1, and *Wentzu:* 1 for *che:snap.* Meanwhile, the standard, Suotan, and Fuyi editions have the puzzling *kung:together,* Wang Pi has the equally strange *ping:army,* and the Mawangtui texts offer no help with *keng:end* and *ching:compete.*

77

天之道。其猶張弓乎。高者抑之。下者舉之。有餘者損之
・不足者補之。天之道。損有餘。而補不足。人之道則
不然。損不足。以奉有餘。孰能有餘。以奉天下。其唯
有道者乎。是以聖人為而不恃。成功而不居。若此其不欲
見賢耶。

The Way of Heaven

is like stringing a bow

pulling down the high

lifting up the low

shortening the long

lengthening the short

the Way of Heaven

takes from the long

and supplements the short

unlike the Way of Man

taking from the short

and giving to the long

who can find the long

and give it to the world

only those who find the Way

thus the sage does not presume on what he does

or claim what he achieves

thus he chooses to hide his skill

KAO HENG says, "In attaching a string to a bow, we pull the bow down to attach the string to the top. We lift the bow up to attach it to the bottom. If the string is too long, we make it shorter. If the string is too short, we make it longer. This is exactly the Way of Heaven." My reading of line two, which agrees with that of Kao Heng, is based on the *Shuowen*, which says, "*Chang* means to attach a string to a bow."

TU ER-WEI says, "Not only the Chinese, but the ancient Greeks and Hindus, the Finns, the Pawnee, the Arapaho all likened the moon to a bow. Thus the Way of Heaven is like a bow" (pp. 97–98).

HO-SHANG KUNG says, "The Way of Heaven is so dark, we need metaphors to understand it. To prepare a bow for use, we string it by pulling down the top and by lifting up the bottom. Likewise, the Way of Heaven takes from the strong and gives to the weak."

LU HUI-CH'ING says, "The Way of Heaven does not intentionally pull down the high and lift up the low. It does nothing and relies instead on the nature of things. Things that are high and long cannot avoid being pulled down and shortened. Things that are low and short cannot avoid being lifted up and lengthened. The full suffer loss. The humble experience gain."

TE-CH'ING says, "The Way of Heaven is to give but not to take. The Way of Man is to take but not to give."

WANG P'ANG says, "The Way of Heaven is based on the natural order. Hence it is fair. The Way of Man is based on desire. Hence it is not fair. Those who possess the Way follow the same Way as Heaven."

SU CH'E says, "Those who possess the Way supply the needs of the ten thousand creatures without saying a word. Only those who possess the Way are capable of this."

LU HSI-SHENG says, "Who can imitate the Way of Heaven and make it the Way of Man, take what one has in abundance and give it to those in need? Only those who possess the Way. The *Yiching* says, 'To take means to take from the low and give to the high (41). To give means to take from the high and give to the low' (42)."

LI JUNG says, "Although the sage performs virtuous deeds, he expects no reward and tries to keep his virtue hidden."

SUNG CH'ANG-HSING says, "The skill of the sage is unfathomable and inexhaustible. How could it be revealed?"

In lines thirteen and fourteen, I have followed the simpler wording of Mawang-tui Text B and the Suotan edition. Lines sixteen and seventeen also appear in verses 2 and 51. For the last line, I have used the briefer Fuyi version.

78

天下莫柔弱於水。而攻堅強者。莫之能先也
。以其無以易之也。柔之勝剛也。弱之勝
強也。天下莫不知。而莫之能行。故聖人
之言云。受邦之垢。是謂社稷之主。受邦之
不祥。是謂天下之王。正言若反。

Nothing in the world is weaker than water
but against the hard and the strong
nothing excels it
for nothing can change it
the soft overcomes the hard
the weak overcomes the strong
this is something everyone knows
but no one is able to practice
thus the sage declares
who accepts a country's disgrace
we call the lord of soil and grain
who accepts a country's misfortune
we call the king of all under Heaven
upright words sound upside down

HSUAN-TSUNG says, "The nature of water is to stay low, not to struggle, and to take on the shape of its container. Thus nothing is weaker. But despite such weakness, it can bore through rocks, while rocks cannot wear down water."

LI HUNG-FU says, "The soft and the weak do not expect to overcome the hard and the strong. They simply do."

HSI T'UNG says, "You can hit it, but you can't hurt it. You can stab it, but you can't wound it. You can hack it, but you can't cut it. You can light it, but you can't burn it. Nothing in the world can alter this thing we call water."

CHU TI-HUANG says, "We can alter the course and shape of water, but we can't alter its basic nature to descend, by means of which it overcomes the hardest and strongest things."

TS'AO TAO-CH'UNG says, "The reason people know this but don't put this into practice is because they love strength and hate weakness."

SUNG CH'ANG-HSING says, "Spies and traitors, thieves and robbers, people who have no respect for the law, disloyal subjects and unfilial children, these are disgraces. Excessive drought and rain, epidemics and locusts, untimely death, famine and homelessness, ominous plants, and misshapen animals, these are misfortunes."

PO-TSUNG says, "Rivers and swamps contain mud. Mountains and marshes harbor diseases. The most beautiful gem has a flaw. The ruler of a state suffers disgrace. This is the Way of Heaven" (*Tsochuan:* Hsuan.15).

SHUN says, "If I commit an offense, it has nothing to do with my people. If my people commit an offense, the offense rests with me" (*Shuching:* 4C.8).

CHUANG-TZU says, "Everyone wants to be first, while I alone want to be last: which means to endure the world's disgrace" (33.5).

MENCIUS says, "If the ruler of a state is not kind, he cannot protect the spirits of the soil and grain" (4A.3).

SU CH'E says, "Upright words agree with the Tao and contradict the world. The world considers enduring disgrace shameful and enduring misfortune a calamity."

LI JUNG says, "The world sees disgrace and innocence, fortune and misfortune. The Taoist sees them all as empty."

KAO YEN-TI says, "The last line sums up the meaning of the abstruse phrases that occur throughout the *Taoteching,* such as 'to act without acting.' The words may contradict, but they complement the truth."

In line four, *yi:change* can also mean "to be easy" (Ho-shang Kung), "to slight" (Li Hung-fu), or "to replace" (Ch'en Ku-ying). In line five, Mawangtui Text B has *shui:water* in place of *jou:soft,* in which case, *kang:hard* would be read "metal." Wu Ch'eng puts the last line at the beginning of the next verse, Yen Tsun combines both verses, and some commentators suggest combining this with verse 43.

79

和大怨。必有餘怨。安可以
為善。是以聖人執左契。而
不以責於人。故有德司契。
無德司徹。天道無親。恆
與善人。

In resolving a great dispute
a dispute is sure to remain
how can this be good
thus the sage holds the left marker
he makes no claim on others
thus the virtuous oversee markers
the virtueless oversee taxes
the Way of Heaven favors no one
but always helps the good

TE-CH'ING says, "In Lao-tzu's day, whenever the feudal rulers had a dispute, the most powerful lord convened a meeting to resolve it. But the resolution of a great dispute invariably involved a payment. And if the payment was not forthcoming, the dispute continued."

WANG PI says, "If we don't arrange a contract clearly, and a dispute results, even using virtuous means to settle it won't restore the injury. Thus a dispute will remain."

SU CH'E says, "If we content ourselves with trimming the branches and don't pull out the roots, things might look fine on the outside, but not on the inside. Disputes come from delusions, and delusions are the product of our nature. Those who understand their nature encounter no delusions, much less disputes."

HO-SHANG KUNG says, "Murderers are killed, and criminals are punished in accordance with their crime. But those who inflict such punishments offend their own human feelings and involve innocent people as well. If even one person sighs, we offend the Heart of Heaven. How can resolving disputes be considered good?"

CH'ENG HSUAN-YING says, "If someone lets go of both sides but still clings to the middle, how can they be completely good?"

SUNG CH'ANG-HSING says, "Seeking to make peace with others is the Way of Man. Not seeking to make peace but letting things make peace by themselves is the Way of Heaven. Despite the expenditure of energy and action, energy and action seldom bring peace. Thus the sage holds the left marker because he relies on inaction and the subtlety of letting things be."

CHENG LIANG-SHU says, "In ancient times, contracts were divided in two. In the state of Ch'u, the creditor kept the left half, and Lao-tzu was from Ch'u. In the central plains, this was reversed, and the creditor kept the right half."

CHIANG HSI-CH'ANG says, "If one does not make demands of others, disputes cannot arise. If one constantly takes from others, great disputes cannot help but occur."

WANG AN-SHIH says, "Those concerned with taxes cannot avoid making claims on others and thus cannot prevent disputes. This is why they lack virtue."

MENCIUS says, "The rulers of the Hsia dynasty exacted a *kung:tribute* on every five acres of land. The rulers of the Shang exacted a *chu:share* on every seven acres. The rulers of the Chou exacted a *ch'e:tax* on every ten acres. In reality, what was paid was a tithe of ten percent" (3A.3). See also *Lunyu:* 12.9.

LU TUNG-PIN says, "Those who are good cultivate themselves. They don't concern themselves with others. Once you concern yourself with others, you have disputes. The good make demands of themselves. They don't make demands of others. The Way of Man is selfish. The Way of Heaven is unselfish. It isn't concerned with others, but it always is one with those who are good."

The last two lines were a common saying. In the *Shuoyuan:* 10.25, they conclude an exhortation to keep still. They also appear in slightly different form in the *Shuching* and in Ch'u Yuan's *Lisao:* "High Heaven favors no one / but it helps the virtuous."

80

小國寡民。使有十百人之器。而不用。使民重死。而不遠
徙。有舟轝。無所乘之。有甲兵。無所陳之。使民復結繩
而用之。甘其食。美其服。安其居。樂其俗。鄰邦相望。
雞狗之聲相聞。民至老死。不相往來。

Imagine a small state with a small population

let there be labor-saving tools

that aren't used

let people consider death

and not move far

let there be boats and carts

but no reason to ride them

let there be armor and weapons

but no reason to employ them

let people return to the use of knots

and be satisfied with their food

and pleased with their clothing

and content with their homes

and happy with their customs

let there be a state so near

people hear its dogs and chickens

and live out their lives

without making a visit

HUANG-TI says, "A great state is *yang*. A small state is *yin*."

SU CH'E says, "Lao-tzu lived during the decline of the Chou, when artifice flourished and customs suffered, and he wished to restore its virtue through doing nothing. Hence at the end of his book he wishes he had a small state to try this on. But he never got his wish."

YAO NAI says, "In ancient times, states were many and small. In later times, they were few and great. But even if a great state wanted to return to the ancient ways, how could it?"

HO-SHANG KUNG says, "Although the sage governs a great state, he thinks of it as a small state and is frugal in the use of its resources. Although the people are many, he thinks of them as few and is careful not to exhaust them."

HU SHIH says, "With the advance of civilization, the power of technology is used to replace human labor. A cart can carry a thousand kilos, and a boat can carry hundreds of passengers. This is the meaning of 'labor-saving tools'" (p. 64).

WANG AN-SHIH says, "When the people are content with their lot, they don't concern themselves with moving far away or going to war."

THE YICHING CHITZU says, "The earliest rulers used knots in their government. Later sages introduced the use of books" (B.2).

WU CH'ENG says, "People who are satisfied with their food and pleased with their clothes cherish their lives and don't tempt death. People who are content with their homes and happy with their customs don't move far away. They grow old and die where they were born."

CH'ENG HSUAN-YING says, "They are satisfied with their food because they taste the Tao. They are pleased with their clothing because they are adorned with virtue. They are content with their homes because they are content everywhere. And they are happy with their customs because they soften the glare of the world."

TS'AO TAO-CH'UNG says, "Those who do their own farming and weaving don't lack food or clothes. They have nothing to give and nothing to seek. Why should they visit others?"

In line two, some editions delete *jen:man* in the compound *shih-po-jen:labor-saving*. I have followed Yen Tsun, Ho-shang Kung, and the Suotan and Mawangtui texts, all of which include it. This phrase can also be interpreted, with or without *jen,* to mean "tools of war." But Hu Shih's reading, seconded by Cheng Liang-shu, is, I think, more profound. After line ten, Ssu-ma Ch'ien and the Fuyi edition add: "the goal of perfect rule / and everyone is . . ." But this appears to be an interpolation. Finally, some editions reverse the order of lines thirteen and fourteen but thereby abandon the rhyme.

81

信言不美。美言不信。善者不辯。辯者不善。知
者不博。博者不知。聖人不積。既以為人。己
愈有。既以與人。己愈多。天之道。利而不害。
聖人之道。為而不爭。

True words aren't beautiful
beautiful words aren't true
the good aren't eloquent
the eloquent aren't good
the wise aren't learned
the learned aren't wise
the sage accumulates nothing
but the more he does for others
the greater his existence
the more he gives to others
the greater his abundance
the Way of Heaven
is to help without harming
the Way of the sage
is to act without struggling

HUANG-TI says, "There is a word for everything. Words that are harmful we say are not true" (*Chingfa: 2*).

TE-CH'ING says, "At the beginning of this book, Lao-tzu says the Tao can't be put into words. But are its 5,000-odd characters not words? Lao-tzu waits until the last verse to explain this. He tells us that though the Tao itself includes no words, by means of words it can be revealed—but only by words that come from the heart."

SU CH'E says, "What is true is real but nothing more. Hence it isn't beautiful. What is beautiful is pleasing to look at but nothing more. Hence it isn't true. Those who focus on goodness don't try to be eloquent, and those who focus on eloquence aren't good. Those who have one thing that links everything together have no need of learning. Those who keep learning don't understand the Tao. The sage holds onto the one and accumulates nothing."

HO-SHANG KUNG says, "True words are simple and not beautiful. The good cultivate the Tao, not the arts. The wise know the Tao, not information. The

162

sage accumulates virtue, not wealth. He gives his wealth to the poor and uses his virtue to teach the unwise. And like the sun or moon, he never stops shining."

CHUANG-TZU says, "When Lao Tan and Yin Hsi heard of people who considered accumulation as deficiency, they were delighted" (33.5).

SUNG CH'ANG-HSING says, "People only worry that their own existence and abundance are insufficient. They don't realize that helping and giving to others does them no harm but brings them benefit instead."

TS'AO TAO-CH'UNG says, "The wealth from giving generously is inexhaustible. The power from not accumulating is boundless."

WU CH'ENG says, "Help is the opposite of harm. Where there is help, there must be harm. But when Heaven helps, it doesn't harm, because it helps without helping. Action is the start of struggle. Where there is action, there must be struggle. But when the sage acts, he doesn't struggle, because he acts without acting."

CHIAO HUNG says, "The past 5,000 words all explain 'the Tao of not accumulating,' what Buddhists call 'non-attachment.' Those who empty their minds on the last two lines will grasp most of Lao-tzu's book."

WANG CHEN says, "The last line summarizes the entire 5,000 words of the previous eighty verses. It doesn't focus on action or inaction but simply on action that doesn't involve struggle.

In lines three and four, the Fuyi edition adds *yen:words*. In the Mawangtui texts, lines three and four are inverted with lines five and six. I haven't used either of these variants, nor have I accepted the variation of the last line introduced by Mawangtui Text B and the Suotan edition, both of which have *jen:man* in place of *sheng-jen:sage*. This would result in "the Way of Man," which does appear in verse 77, but in a pejorative sense.

Glossary

In addition to proper names and Chinese terms, the following list includes the names and dates of all commentators quoted in the preceding pages along with the titles of texts from which I have quoted selected passages.

Chang Tao-ling 張道陵 (34–157 AD). Patriarch of the Way of Celestial Masters, the earliest-known Taoist movement, which emphasized physical and moral training as well as spiritual cultivation. His commentary was lost until a partial copy, including verses 3 through 37, was found in the Tunhuang Caves: s.6825. *Lao-tzu hsiang-erh-chu.*

Chankuotse 戰國策. Collection of narratives, some historical, some fictional, based on the events of the Warring States Period (403–221 BC). Compiled by Liu Hsiang (c. 79–6 BC) and re-edited by later scholars.

Ch'en Ku-ying 陳鼓應 (1935–). Classical scholar and philosopher who has taught in Taipei and Peking and annoyed authorities in both places with his outspoken views. *Lao-tzu chu-yi chi-p'ing-chieh.*

Ch'eng Chu 程俱 (1078–1144). Scholar-official and fearless critic of government policies with which he did not agree. *Lao-tzu-lun.*

Ch'eng Hsuan-ying 成玄英 (fl. 647–663). Taoist master and proponent of using an eclectic approach to explain the teachings of Lao-tzu. His commentary, recently re-edited from portions in the Taoist Canon and Tunhuang manuscript S.2517, reflects the influence of Chuang-tzu along with Buddhist Sanlun and Tientai teachings. It was required reading for Taoists seeking ordination during the T'ang dynasty. *Lao-tzu-shu.*

Cheng Liang-shu 鄭良樹 (1940–). Classical scholar and leading authority on the Mawangtui texts. His presentation of differences between the Mawangtui and other editions appears in *Ta-lu tsa-chih* vols. 54–59 (April 1977–October 1979). His study of Tunhuang copies of the *Taoteching* is also excellent: *Lao-tzu lun-chi.*

Chiang Hsi-ch'ang 蔣錫昌 (publ. 1937). *Lao-tzu chiao-chieh.*

Ch'iang Ssu-ch'i 強思齊 (fl. 920). Taoist master of the Former Shu dynasty (Szechuan province) during the Five Dynasties period. His edition is invaluable for its preservation of the comments of Li Jung, Ch'eng Hsuan-ying, and Yen Tsun, as well as those of Hsuan-tsung and Ho-shang Kung. *Tao-te-chen-ching hsuan-te-tsuan-shu.*

Chiao Hung 焦竑 (1541–1620). Noted compiler of bibliographic works. His 1587 edition of the *Taoteching* includes his own occasional comments as well as selected commentaries of mostly Sung dynasty authors, especially Su Ch'e, Lu Hui-ch'ing, and Li Hsi-chai. It remains one of the most useful such compilations. *Lao-tzu-yi.*

Chieh 桀 (d. 1766 BC) and Chou 紂 (d. 1122 BC). Tyrants whose reigns concluded the Hsia and Shang dynasties respectively.

Chingfu 景福. Inscription of the *Taoteching* carved in the second year of the Chingfu period (893) at Lunghsing Temple in Yichou, southwest of Peking.

Chinglung 景龍. Inscription of the *Taoteching* carved in the second year of the Chinglung period (708) also at Yichou's Lunghsing Temple. Authorities in charge of the temple's former site have no idea what happened to these two stelae, though several elderly village women told me they were moved south to another county in the same province—they didn't know which county or when the move took place. A third *Taoteching* stele, carved in 738, is the lone survivor of Lunghsing Temple's collection of ancient inscriptions.

Chinjenming 金人銘. An inscription that Confucius reports seeing on the back of a metal statue whose mouth was papered over. The statue, he says, was at the entrance to an early Chou dynasty shrine to Houchi, the God of Crops. (*Kungtzu Chiayu:* 11). A copy of the inscription now stands near the entrance to the Duke of Chou's shrine in Confucius's home town of Chufu.

Chu Ch'ien-chih 朱謙之 (1899–1972). Classical scholar and teacher of philosophy and history. His edition of the *Taoteching* presents variants, rhymes, and usages, along with his own comments. *Lao-tzu chiao-shih.*

Chu Ti-huang 朱蒂煌 (1885–1941). Ch'ing dynasty official and early revolutionary. After fleeing the country, he returned to China to devote himself to Buddhism and Chinese philosophy.

Ch'u Yuan 屈原 (340?–278 BC). China's first great poet and author of the *Lisao.*

His suicide in the Milo River is now celebrated on the fifth day of the fifth moon as Poet's Day and marked by dragon boat races to save his body from the fishes.

Chuang-tzu 莊子 (369–286 BC). After Lao-tzu, the greatest of the early Taoist philosophers. The work that bears his name contains some of the most imaginative examples of early Chinese writing and includes numerous quotes from the *Taoteching*. The work was added to by later writers and edited into its present form by Kuo Hsiang (d. 312).

Chungyung 中庸 (*Doctrine of the Mean*). Attributed to Tzu-ssu, the grandson of Confucius. It forms part of a larger work known as the *Lichi*, or *Book of Rites*.

Confucius 孔夫子 (551–479 BC). China's most revered teacher of doctrines emphasizing the harmony of human relations. His teachings, along with those of his disciples, were compiled into the *Lunyu* (*Analects*), the *Chungyung* (*Doctrine of the Mean*), and the *Tahsueh* (*Great Learning*) and until recently formed the basis of moral education in China.

Diamond Sutra 金剛經 (*Vajracchedika Prajnaparamita Sutra*). Along with the shorter *Heart Sutra* and the longer *Lotus Sutra*, this is one of the most popular of all Buddhist texts. It was first translated into Chinese by Kumarajiva around 400 AD.

Duke Ai 哀公 (fl. fifth cent. BC). Ruler of the state of Lu and interlocutor of *Lunyu*: 12.9.

Duke Wen of Chin 晉文公 (fl. seventh cent. BC). Ruler of the state of Chin and hegemon of the central states.

Fan Ying-yuan 范應元 (fl. 1240–1269). One of the first scholars to examine variations in pronunciation and wording in the *Taoteching*. *Lao-tzu tao-te-ching ku-pen-chi-chu*.

Five Emperors 五帝. According to the lineage of Ssu-ma Ch'ien, they included Shao Hao (c. 2600–2500 BC), Chuan Hsu (c. 2500–2400 BC), Ti K'u (c. 2400–2350 BC), Yao (c. 2350–2250 BC), and Shun (c. 2250–2150 BC).

Fu Hsi 伏羲 (c. 3500 BC). Sage ruler of prehistoric times and the reputed inventor of the system of hexagrams on which the *Yiching* is based.

Fuyi 傅奕. Copy of the *Taoteching* that came to light in 574 near the town of Hsuchou in the grave of one of the concubines of Hsiang Yu. Although the date of her death is unknown, Hsiang Yu died in 202 BC. Along with the Mawangtui texts, which date from the same period, this constitutes one of the earliest known copies. Fu Yi (555–639) was a court astrologer and outspoken opponent of Buddhist monasticism who published the text along with his own commentary. Subsequent editions of the text suggest he made some minor changes involving grammatical particles. *Fu-yi chiao-ting ku-pen-lao-tzu.*

Han Fei 韓非 (d. 233 BC). Student of the Confucian philosopher, Hsun-tzu. His collection of rhetoric and antecdotes, known as the *Hanfeitzu,* is noted for its Legalist philosophy. Chapters 20 and 21 consist of numerous quotes from the *Taoteching* and include commentaries on verses 38, 46, 50, 53, 54, 58, 59, 60, and 67. Although Han Fei often misconstrues phrases to support his own ideas, his is the earliest-known commentary.

Hanku Pass 函谷關. A 17-kilometer-long defile through the loess plateau on the border between Honan and Shensi provinces. Lao-tzu reportedly conveyed to the Warden of the Pass the text that makes up the *Taoteching.*

Ho-shang Kung 河上公 (d. 159 BC?). Taoist master who lived in a hut beside the Yellow River—hence his name, which means "Master Riverside." His commentary emphasizes Taoist yoga and was reportedly composed at the request of Emperor Wen (179–156 BC). It ranks next to that of Wang Pi in popularity. Some scholars think it originated in the third or fourth century AD from the Taoist lineage that included Ko Hung (283–343). There is at least one English translation: Eduard Erkes, Artibus Asiae (Switzerland), 1950. *Lao-tzu-chu.*

Houhanshu 後漢書 (*History of the Latter Han Dynasty*). Compiled by Fan Yeh (398–445) for the period 25–220 AD.

Hsi T'ung 奚侗 (1876–1936). Official and classical scholar known for his commentaries on the philosophical texts of the Warring States period (403–221 BC). *Lao-tzu chi-chieh.*

Hsin Tu-tzu 心都子. Interlocutor in *Liehtzu*: 8.25.

Hsishengching 西升經 (*Book of the Western Ascension*). Taoist work apparently composed during the first centuries AD. It is one of several texts that recount Lao-tzu's reappearance in India following his transmission of the *Taoteching* to Yin Hsi.

Hsu Yung-chang 許永璋 (publ. 1992). Hsu's commentary, which took forty years to publish, is prefaced by a thorough and wide-ranging discussion of the *Taoteching* as poetry. *Lao-tzu shih-hsueh yu-chou.*

Hsuan-tsung 玄宗 (Li Lung-chi 李隆基) (r. 712–762). One of China's greatest emperors. He was also a skilled poet and calligrapher and deeply interested in Taoism as well as Buddhism. I have quoted from his own commentary, written in 732, as well as from another commentary compiled under his direction that expands on his earlier effort. *Yu-chu tao-te-chen-ching* and *Yu-chih tao-te-chen-ching-shu.*

Hsueh Hui 薛蕙 (1489–1541). Official, classical scholar, and student of the occult. His work on the *Taoteching* is notable for its critical review of previous commentaries. *Lao-tzu chi-chieh* and *Lao-tzu k'ao-yi.*

Hsun-tzu 荀子 (fl. 300–240 BC). Teacher of Han Fei as well as Li Ssu, the First Emperor's infamous prime minister. He is considered the third of the great Confucian philosophers, after Confucius and Mencius, though his rationalism is often at odds with their idealism. His teachings are contained in a book of essays that bears his name.

Hu Shih 胡適 (1891–1962). Student of John Dewey and leader of the New Culture Movement that helped establish vernacular Chinese as a legitimate form of literary expression. *Chung-kuo che-hsueh-shih ta-kang.*

Huai-nan-tzu 淮南子 (Liu An 劉安) (d. 122 BC). Grandson of Liu Pang, the first Han emperor. He was a devoted Taoist, although his search for the elixir of immortality was prematurely interrupted when he was accused of plotting to succeed to the throne and forced to commit suicide. The book that bears his title is a collection of treatises on mostly Taoist themes written by a group of scholars at his court.

Huang Mao-ts'ai 黃茂村 (fl. 1174–90). Scholar and military official. *Lao-tzu-chieh.*

Huang Yuan-chi 黃元吉 (fl. 1820–1874). Taoist master famous for his sermons and oral exposition of Taoist texts. His commentary, which he dictated to a disciple, focuses on internal yoga as well as on points in common between the teachings of Lao-tzu and Confucius. *Tao-te-ching ching-yi.*

Huang-ti 黃帝 (Yellow Emperor) (c. 2700–2600 BC). The patriarch (some now say matriarch) of Chinese civilization and leader of the confederation of tribes that established themselves along the Yellow River. When excavators opened the Mawangtui tombs, they also found four previously unknown texts attributed to Huang-ti: *Chingfa, Shihtaching, Cheng,* and *Taoyuan.*

Huangti Neiching 黃帝內經 (*Internal Treatise of the Yellow Emperor*). Earliest known text on Chinese medicine. It records conversations between the Yellow Emperor and his physician, Ch'i Po. What appears to be the long-lost *External Treatise* was also found in the Mawangtui tombs.

Huhsien 苦縣. Established as a prefecture during the Chou dynasty, at first as part of the state of Ch'en and later as part of the state of Ch'u. According to Ssu-ma Ch'ien, Lao-tzu was born in the village of Chujen, just outside the prefectural seat. A shrine still marks the location of the former village.

Hui-tsung 徽宗 (Chao Chi 趙佶) (r. 1101–1125). Sung dynasty emperor and one of China's greatest calligraphers and patrons of the arts. His commentary was finished in 1118, shortly before he was taken captive by nomad invaders. *Yu-chieh tao-te-chen-ching.*

Jen Chi-yu 任繼愈 (1916–). Professor of religion and philosophy at Peking University. His many publications include an English translation of the *Taoteching*. *Lao-tzu che-hsueh t'ao-lun-chi.*

Jen Fa-jung. 任法融 (1930–). Current abbot of Loukuantai, the Taoist center where Lao-tzu reportedly wrote the *Taoteching*. Master Jen has been publicly critical of state control of religious sites, and his is the only commentary I know of by a Taoist monk subsequent to the Cultural Revolution. *Tao-te-ching shih-yi.*

Kao Heng 高亨 (1900–). Classical scholar and advocate of using grammatical analysis to elucidate textual difficulties in the *Taoteching*. Many of his insights have been borne out by the texts discovered at Mawangtui. *Lao-tzu cheng-ku.*

Kao Yen-ti 高延第 (1823–1886). Classical scholar and member of the Hanlin Academy. In addition to providing several unique interpretations of his own, his commentary cites passages of the *Taoteching* that appear in other ancient texts. *Lao-tzu cheng-yi.*

King Hsiang of Liang 梁襄王 (fl. fourth cent. BC). Ruler of the small state of Liang (modern Kaifeng) and son of King Hui.

Ku Hsi-ch'ou 顧錫疇 (fl. 1600–1630). Scholar-official. His is one of several commentaries incorrectly attributed to the T'ang-dynasty Taoist, Lu Tung-pin. *Tao-te-ching-chieh.*

Kuan Lung-feng 關龍逄 (c. 1800 BC). Prime Minister during the reign of Emperor Chieh, last emperor of the Hsia dynasty. Chieh had Kuan killed for his unwelcome advice.

Kuan-tzu 管子 (d. 645 BC). Prime minister of the state of Ch'i. The voluminous work that bears his name more likely incorporates the views of the Chi-hsia Academy that flourished in the Ch'i capital about the same time.

Kumarajiva 鳩摩羅什 (344–413). Native of the Silk Road kingdom of Kucha and greatest of all translators of Buddhist scriptures into Chinese. *Lao-tzu-chu.*

Kuo Yen 郭偃 (fl. seventh cent. BC). Chief minister of the state of Chin during the reign of Duke Wen.

Kuoyu 國語 (*Dialogues of the States*). Like the *Tsochuan,* with which it overlaps and shares much material, this is a compilation of Chou dynasty history and fictional narrative focusing primarily on the period 770–464 BC. Traditionally, but erroneously, attributed to Tso Ch'iu-ming.

Kushihyuan 古詩原. Anthology of pre-T'ang dynasty poetry compiled by Shen Te-ch'ien (1673–1769) and published in 1719.

Li Hsi-chai 李息齋 (fl. 1167). Taoist master, practitioner of Taoist yoga, and noted *Yiching* scholar. His commentary extends Lao-tzu's teachings to the state as well as to the individual. *Tao-te-chen-ching yi-chieh.*

Li Hung-fu 李宏甫 (fl. 1574). His commentary can be found appended to a re-issue of Su Ch'e's commentary. In his preface, he says the differences between Confucius and Lao-tzu are no more significant than the preference for wheat in North China and rice in the South. *Lao-tzu-chieh.*

Li Jung 李榮 (fl. 670). Taoist master and proponent of the Chunghsuan (Double-Darkness) approach to the truth that first uses darkness to break through the dialectic of darkness and light and then renounces darkness as well. His commentary has been recently re-edited from portions that survive in the Taoist canon as well as from several Tunhuang copies. *Tao-te-chen-ching-chu.*

Li Yueh 李約 (fl. 683). Military official, accomplished poet, calligrapher, and painter of the plum tree. He viewed the Confucian classics as no more than leaves and branches and the *Taoteching* as the root. *Tao-te-chen-ching hsin-chu.*

Lichi 禮記 (*Book of Rites*). Anthology of Confucian writings, including the *Chungyung* and the *Tahsueh.* It was first put together around the second century BC and further edited by Tai Te and his cousin during the following century.

Lieh-tzu 列子 (fl. fourth century BC). Taoist master about whom nothing is known, other than that he could ride the wind. The book that bears his name was probably the work of his disciples and later generations of Taoists. The present version dates from the fifth century AD.

Lin Hsi-yi 林希逸 (fl. 1234–60). Scholar-official who produced commentaries to a number of classics. His commentary on the *Taoteching* is noted for its clarity. *Lao-tzu k'ou-yi.*

Liu Ch'en-weng 劉辰翁 (1232–1297). Poet and essayist. He held several official posts but spent most of his life in obscurity, if not seclusion. *Lao-tzu tao-te-ching p'ing-tien.*

Liu Ching 劉涇 (fl. 1074). Recognized for his literary talent by Wang An-shih, he was given several minor posts but failed to advance due to his fondness for argument. *Lao-tzu-chu.*

Liu Chung-p'ing 劉仲平 (fl. 1060). Official and member of Wang An-shih's reform clique. *Lao-tzu-chu.*

Liu Pang 劉邦 (247–195 BC). Helped overthrow the Ch'in dynasty and became the first emperor of the Han dynasty.

Liu Shih-li 劉師立 (fl. 1200). *Lao-tzu-chieh-chieh.*

Liu Shih-p'ei 劉師培 (1884–1919). Adds to the work of Wang Nien-sun and others in locating ancient usages. *Lao-tzu-chiao-pu.*

Lo Chen-yu 羅振玉 (1866–1940). Archaeologist, educator, bibliographer, agronomist, advisor to the last emperor, and among the first scholars to study the Tunhuang copies of the *Taoteching. Tao-te-ching k'ao-yi* and *Tun-huang-pen lao-tzu yi-ts'an-chuan.*

Lu Hsi-sheng 陸希聲 (fl. 890). High official and scholar known for his wide learning. His commentary reflects the view that Lao-tzu and Confucius were the spiritual heirs of Fu Hsi (c. 3500 BC), with Lao-tzu emphasizing the *yin* and Confucius the *yang* aspects of the Way of Heaven. *Tao-te-chen-ching-chuan.*

Lu Hui-ch'ing 呂惠卿 (1031–1111). Gifted writer selected by Wang An-shih to help draft his reform proposals. His commentary, presented to the emperor in 1078, is quoted at length by Chiao Hung. *Tao-te-chen-ching-chuan.*

Lu Nung-shih 陸農師 (1042–1102). High official and scholar known for his knowledge of ritual usage. His commentary makes extensive use of quotes from *Liehtzu* and *Chuangtzu. Lao-tzu-chu.*

Lu Tung-pin 呂洞賓 (fl. 845). Leader of the legendary Eight Immortals and author of a number of Taoist works, including *Secret of the Golden Flower.* Several commentaries have been attributed to him. I have used the *Tao-te-ching shih-yi.*

Lushih Chunchiu 呂氏春秋 (*The Spring and Autumn Annals of Mr. Lu*). Commissioned by Lu Pu-wei (d. 235 BC), this was probably the first Chinese text written with a unified plan. It purported to contain all that anyone needed to know of the world and was Taoist in conception. Not to be confused with *The Spring and Autumn Annals of Master Yen* or *The Spring and Autumn Annals* written in the state of Lu and attributed to Confucius.

Ma Hsu-lun 馬敘倫 (1884–1970). Minister of Education, member of several legislative bodies, and classical scholar. One of the first scholars to suggest rearranging passages of the *Taoteching* to remedy inconsistencies which he thought were the result of inadvertant shuffling of the wooden strips on which the text was first written. *Lao-tzu chiao-ku.*

Mawangtui 馬王堆. Suburb of Changsha, capital of Hunan province, and the site of several Han dynasty graves that were excavated in 1973–4. Among the contents of one of the graves were two copies of the *Taoteching* written on silk. Although the grave was sealed in 168 BC, the presence or absence of certain characters proscribed after the onset of the Han dynasty suggest that Text A was copied before 206 BC and Text B was copied between 206 and 194 BC. Along with the Fuyi text, they constitute our earliest copies of the *Taoteching*. One noteworthy difference in the Mawangtui texts is the re-ordering of several verses and the placement of the second half of the text first.

Mencius 孟子 (390–305 BC). Ranked with Confucius and Hsun-tzu as one of the foremost teachers of the philosophy known as Confucianism. He studied with Confucius' grandson, Tzu-ssu. The work that bears his name records his conversations with his disciples and various rulers.

Ming T'ai-tsu 明太祖 (Chu Yuan-chang 朱元璋) (1328–1398). Grew up in a family of destitute farmers, became a Buddhist monk, joined a rebellion against the Mongols (who had occupied the Chinese throne since 1278), and founded the Ming dynasty (1368–1644). His commentary, which he apparently wrote without the help of tutors, was completed in 1374. *Tao-te-chen-ching yu-chu.*

Mo-tzu 墨子 (fl. fifth cent. BC). Philosopher whose arguments in favor of universal love and against costly funerals put him at odds with the Confucian school, especially Mencius and Hsun-tzu. The work that bears his name was apparently composed after his death by his disciples, who themselves betray differences of opinion concerning their master's views.

Mou-tzu 牟子 (Mou Jung 牟融) (fl. third cent.). High official and author of the *Lihuolun*, the earliest-known work that addresses the problems arising from Buddhist practice and Chinese tradition.

Pao-ting庖丁. Knife-wielding cook of *Chuangtzu: 3.2*.

Pi Kan比干 (fl. 1150 BC). Advisor to the last emperor of the Shang dynasty, who had Pi killed for his frank counsel.

Pi Yuan 畢沅 (1730–1797). Prominent scholar-official with interests in history, philology, and geography. *Lao-tzu tao-te-ching k'ao-yi*.

Po-tsung伯宗 (fl. eighth cent. BC). Minister at the court of Chin. His views are reported in the *Tsochuan:* Hsuan.15.

Shanhaiching 山海經 (*Book of Mountains and Seas*). Shaman's guide to China's mountains and waterways. Attributed to Yu the Great (fl. 2200 BC), it was edited into its present form by Liu Hsin (c. 50 BC–23 AD). A reliable English translation was published by Taiwan's National Institute for Compilation and Translation in 1985.

Shao Juo-yu 邵若愚 (fl. 1135–70). *Tao-te-chen-ching chih-chieh*.

Shen Nung 神晨 (c. 2800–2700 BC). Legendary ruler of China's prehistoric period. He is venerated as the father of agriculture and herbal medicine in China.

Shihching 詩經. Collection of some 300 poems from China's earliest historical period, between the twelfth and seventh century BC. Arranged by style and region, it was reportedly compiled by Confucius from a larger corpus of over 3,000 poems. It remained an essential part of traditional education until the twentieth century.

*Shuching*書經. Collection of memorials from China's earliest historical period: the Hsia, Shang, and Chou dynasties. Reputedly edited by Confucius, there are two versions, one of which contains 28 chapters and which most scholars think is genuine and another with an additional 22 chapters of debatable authenticity.

Shun 舜 (c. 2250–2150 BC). Early sage ruler noted for his filial piety and non-interference in public affairs.

*Shuowen*說文 Greatest of China's early etymological dictionaries. It was compiled and first published by Hsu Shen in 121 AD and revised and updated with new materials in the T'ang, Sung, and Ch'ing dynasties.

*Shuoyuan*說苑 Collection of moral tales and political discourses. Attributed to Liu Hsiang (c. 79–6 BC), who also compiled the *Chankuotse*.

Ssu-ma Ch'ien 司馬遷 (145–85 BC). Together with his father, Ssu-ma T'an, author of the first comprehensive history of China. His biography of Lao-tzu

Tomb of Su Ch'e (Su Tzu-yu). Located in Honan province near the town of Juchou. Beyond Su's grave are the graves of his father and his more famous brother, Su Tung-p'o. Photo by Bill Porter.

constitutes the earliest known record of the Taoist patriarch. *Shih-chi* (*Records of the Historian*): 63.

Ssu-ma Kuang 司馬光 (1019–1086). One of the most famous writers and political figures of the Sung dynasty and adversary of Wang An-shih. His multi-volume history of China remains one of the most thorough treatments of China's past through the T'ang dynasty. His commentary interprets Lao-tzu's text using Confucian terminology and Neo-Confucian concepts. *Tao-te-chen-ching-lun.*

Su Ch'e 蘇轍 (1039–1112). Along with his father and brother, he was one of the eight great prose writers of the T'ang and Sung dynasties. Although his commentary reflects his own Neo-Confucian sympathies, it is treasured by Buddhists and Taoists alike. *Tao-te-chen-ching-chu.*

Suichou 遂州. Inscription of the *Taoteching* carved during the T'ang dynasty at Suichou's Lunghsing Temple. Not dated.

Sung Ch'ang-hsing 宋常星 (fl. 1700). Taoist master and seventh patriarch of the Dragon Gate sect of the Golden Lotus lineage. His commentary on the *Taoteching* was a favorite of Emperor K'ang-hsi (r. 1662–1722). *Tao-te-ching chiang*-yi.

Sun-tzu 孫子 (fl. 512 BC). Master of military tactics and strategy. His *Pingfa,* or *Art of War,* has been much studied and admired ever since it came to the attention of King Ho Lu of the state of Wu, who subsequently became Sun's patron.

Suotan 索紞. Partial copy of the *Taoteching,* including verses 51 through 81, found in the Tunhuang Caves. It was copied on paper in 270 AD by Suo Tan, a Tunhuang native famous for his prognostication of dreams. Although it was not included in early Tunhuang catalogues, it has been verified and re-copied by Yeh Chien-ting and Huang Pin-hung. Formerly in the collection of Li Mu-chai, it is currently in the possession of Chang Chun.

Sweet dew 甘露. Name for the saliva produced during meditation by pressing the tongue against the roof of the mouth. An essential element in the creation of a pure body capable of transcending death.

Tahsueh 大學 (*Great Learning*). One of the Confucian classics. It was later included as part of the *Lichi,* or *Book of Rites.* Some scholars attribute its composition to Confucius' disciple Tseng-tzu, while others think it was written by his grandson, Tzu-ssu.

Te-ch'ing 德清 (Han-shan 憨山) (1546–1623). One of the greatest Buddhist writers of the Ming dynasty. Although he was a devoted follower and popularizer of Buddhist Pure Land practice, his commentaries on Lao-tzu and Chuang-tzu reveal exceptional insight. *Lao-tzu tao-te-ching-chieh.*

Three Sovereigns 三皇. Fu Hsi (c. 3500 BC), Shen Nung (c. 2800–2700 BC), and Huang-ti (c. 2700–2600 BC), the Yellow Emperor.

Ts'ao Tao-ch'ung 曹道沖 (fl. Sung dynasty: 960–1278). Taoist nun. *Lao-tzu-chu.*

Tseng-tzu 曾子 (b. 505 BC). Disciple of Confucius and author of the *Hsiaoching,* or *Book of Piety.* His views are also quoted at length in the *Lunyu* and the *Tahsueh.*

Tsochuan 左傳 (*Annals of Tso*). First comprehensive account of the major political events of the Spring and Autumn Period (722–481 BC). It was compiled during the fourth century BC by Tso Ch'iu-ming, about whom we know nothing else.

Tu Er-wei 杜而未 (1913–1987). Scholar of Chinese religion and comparative mythology and a proponent of the view that Taoism had its origin in the worship of the moon. *Lao-tzu-te yueh-shen tsung-chiao.*

Tu Tao-chien 杜道堅 (fl. 1264–1306). Taoist master and author of commentaries to a number of Taoist classics. His *Taoteching* commentary makes extensive use of quotes from the Confucian classics. *Tao-te-hsuan-ching yuan-chih.*

Tung Ssu-ching 董思靖 (fl. 1246–1257). Taoist master and compiler of Taoist texts in the Ling-pao tradition. His commentary includes extensive quotes from T'ang and Sung dynasty commentators as well as his own comments. *Tao-te-chen-ching chi-chieh.*

Tunhuang 敦煌. China's westernmost outpost on the Silk Road as early as the Han dynasty and the location of dozens of Buddhist devotional caves carved into a hillside from the fourth through the fourteenth centuries. At the end of the nineteenth century, a Taoist caretaker opened a sealed side-room in one of the caves and found more than 30,000 manuscripts, most of which dated from the eighth through the eleventh century. From 1907 onward, he began selling these manuscripts to collectors, and the majority ended up in the national archives of France and England. Although most were Buddhist sutras, they included at least 60 copies of various portions of the *Taoteching.*

Tzu-ssu 子思 (d. 483 BC). Grandson of Confucius and author of the *Chungyung.*

Wang An-shih 王安石 (1021–1086). One of China's most famous prime ministers. His attempt to introduce sweeping reforms directed against merchants and landowners galvanized Chinese intellectuals into a debate that continues to this day. He was also one of the great poets and prose writers of his day. His commentary has been re-edited from scattered sources by Yen Ling-feng. *Lao-tzu-chu.*

Wang Chen 王真 (fl. 809). T'ang dynasty general and student of the *Taoteching.* His commentary, which he presented to Emperor Hsiuan Tsung, remains unique for its display of pacificist sympathies by a military official. *Tao-te-ching lun-ping yao-yi-shu*

Wang Nien-sun 王念孫 (1744–1832). Distinguished philologist whose analysis of grammatical particles used in ancient texts is unrivalled. His approach is also unique in not taking characters at their face value but in viewing them as possible homophones. *Lao-tzu tsa-chih.*

Wang P'ang 王雱 (1044–1076). Brilliant scholar, writer, and son of Wang An-shih. His commentary, written in 1070, was "lost" until Yen Ling-feng re-edited it from scattered sources. *Lao-tzu-chu.*

Wang Pi王弼 (226–249 AD). Famous for the quickness of his mind as well as the breadth of his learning, he grew up with one of the best private libraries of his time. Although he died of a sudden illness at the age of twenty-four, he was among the first to discuss Taoism as metaphysics rather than religion. As a result, his commentary has been preferred over that of Ho-shang Kung by Confucian scholars. At least two English translations exist: Paul Lin, University of Michigan Center for Chinese Studies, 1977; Ariane Rump, University of Hawaii Press, 1979. *Lao-tzu-chu.*

Wang Tao 王道 (1476–1532). Incorporates Confucian interpretations in his commentary. *Lao-tzu-yi.*

Wang Wu-chiu 王無咎 (fl. 1056). Scholar-official. He gave up a promising official career in order to devote himself to studying and teaching. *Lao-tzu-yi.*

Wei Yuan 魏源 (1794–1856). Classicist, historian, geographer, and admired administrator. While his own views are insightful, his commentary consists largely in selections from Chiao Hung's edition. *Lao-tzu pen-yi.*

Wen-tzu 文子 (fl. fifth cent. BC). Taoist recluse and teacher of Fan Li, prime minister of the state of Yueh. According to the *Hanshu,* he was a disciple of Lao-tzu and a contemporary of Confucius. The book that bears his name is attributed to his disciples.

Wu Ch'eng 吳澄 (1249–1333). One of the great prose writers of the Yuan dynasty, surpassed only by his student, Yu Chi (1272–1348). His commentary shows exceptional insight and provides unique background information. It is also noted for its division of the text into 68 verses. *Tao-te-chen-ching-chu.*

Yang 陽. The bright side, the male, the strong.

Yang Hsiung 揚雄 (53 BC–18 AD). Gifted writer of courtly odes and philosopher. Known for his view that man is neither good nor bad by nature but wholly subject to his environment. A number of his odes are preserved in the *Wenhsuan.* The *Fayen* contains his philosophical maxims.

Yao Nai 姚鼐 (1732–1815). One of the most famous literary figures of the Ch'ing dynasty and advocate of writing in the style of ancient prose. His anthology of ancient literary models, *Kuwentzu Leitsuan,* has had a great influence on writers and remains in use. *Lao-tzu chang-chu.*

Yellow Emperor (Huang-ti 黃帝) (c. 2700–2600 BC). Patriarch of Chinese culture. He was also among the earliest known practitioners of Taoist yoga and other hygienic arts.

Yen Fu 嚴復 (1853–1921). Naval officer, scholar, and the first Chinese commentator to use Western philosophical concepts in interpreting Lao-tzu. *Lao-tzu tao-te-ching p'ing-tien.*

Yen Ling-feng 嚴靈峰 (1910–). Classical scholar and specialist in *Taoteching* studies. In addition to his own books on the subject, he re-published most of the surviving commentaries in his monumental *Wu-ch'iu-pei-chai lao-tzu chi-ch'eng,* including a number of "lost" commentaries which he re-edited from scattered sources. *Lao-tzu chang-chu hsin-pien.*

Yen Tsun 嚴遵 (Chun-p'ing 君平) (fl. 53–24 BC). Urban recluse of Chengtu. He supported himself as a fortune-teller and spent his remaining time reading and pondering the *Taoteching.* The lengthy commentaries that he produced are sometimes quite profound but more often obscure, and those that survive are incomplete. He divides the text into 72 verses. *Tao-te-ching chih-kuei.*

Yentiehlun 鹽鐵論 (*Discource on Salt and Iron*). Record of debates on government policies and other problems of the day compiled by Huan K'uan (fl. 73 BC).

Yiching 易經 (*Book of Changes*). Ancient manual of divination based on a system of hexagrams invented by Fu Hsi (c. 3500 BC) with judgments attributed to Duke Wen and the Duke of Chou (c. 1200–1100 BC), and commentaries added some 600 years later, ostensibly by Confucius.

Yiching Chitzu. 易經繫辭 (*Appended Judgments on the Yiching*). Attributed to Duke Wen.

Yin 陰. The dark side, the female, the weak.

Yin Hsi 尹喜 (fl. sixth cent. BC). Taoist astronomer who met Lao-tzu at Hanku Pass and to whom Lao-tzu subsequently conveyed the *Taoteching.* Several works have been attributed to him, though those that survive are probably by later Taoists.

Yin Wen 尹文 (350–284 BC). Eclectic philosopher of the state of Ch'i and author of a book of discourses that bears his name.

Yu Juo 有若 (fl. fifth cent. BC). Disciple of Confucius known for his resemblence to the sage as well as for his love of antiquity. After Confucius's death, many of his disciples wanted to render to Yu Juo the same observances they had conferred on Confucius. But this was opposed by Tseng-tzu.

Yunchi Chichien 雲笈七籤. Anthology of Taoist writings edited by Chang Chun-fang (fl. 1017–21). One of the most influential such compilations, it is also called the Shorter Taoist Canon.

Sung dynasty stele at the grave of Lao-tzu's mother. Photo by Bill Porter.

On the Spelling
of Chinese Names

A modified Wade-Giles system, in which umlauts have been omitted, is used throughout. According to this system, aspirated consonants are unvoiced ("t'" is pronounced "t" as in "toy," and "ch'" is pronounced "ch" as in "church"). Unaspirated consonants are voiced ("t" is pronounced "d" as in "dog" and "ch" is pronounced "j" as in "jam"). The only unusual pronunciation is "j," which is pronounced "r" as "row." And the only vowel that is pronounced differently from what one might expect in English is the final "e" or "u," which is given little or no emphasis. Thus the "tzu" in "Lao-tzu" is pronounced the same as the final part of the word "adze." For the names of places and books, I have omitted the apostrophes and hyphens and run words together. Thus Tao-te-ching becomes *Taoteching*, and Lao-tzu the person becomes *Laotzu* the book. I have also retained commonly used spellings based on other romanization systems. Thus, Yangtze instead of Changchiang.

Acknowledgments

The translator is indebted to Michael O'Connor and Christina McLennan for critical readings of the English text, to Paul Hansen for his fine map, to Steven R. Johnson for his photo of the Mawangtui texts, to Martin Merz for help in China, and to Paul Hansen, Jack Estes, Fred Goforth, Nicholas Gould, and the U. S. Department of Agriculture's Food Stamp program for various forms of financial assistance.

Cover, interior design in Dante and Columbus, and typesetting by Thomas Christensen. Chinese characters typeset by Katherine Loh Design. Map on p. viii by Paul Hansen. Edited by Thomas Christensen and Kirsten Janene-Nelson, with assistance from Victoria Bullman, Sarah Fallon, and Jürgen Möllers; proofread by Catherine Park. Printing and binding by Data Reproductions, using fifty-five–pound Glatefelter Opaque recycled paper.

道

The cover and title page calligraphy of the character *Tao* 道 is by one of China's greatest calligraphers, Yen Chen-ch'ing 顏真卿 (709–785). It is part of a longer inscription written circa 775 at the Taoist center of Maoshan 茅山 while Yen was Military Commissioner of the Huchou area.